Other titles in the series:

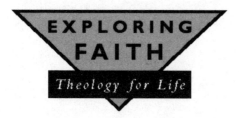

EXPLORING
FAITH
Theology for Life

SERIES EDITORS: Leslie J Francis and Jeff Astley

EXPLORING GOD-TALK

Using Language in Religion

Jeff Astley

DARTON·LONGMAN +TODD

First published in 2004 by
Darton, Longman and Todd Ltd
1 Spencer Court
140-142 Wandsworth High Street
London SW18 4JJ

ISBN 0-232-52519-6

A catalogue record for this book is available from the British Library.

Typeset by Intype Libra Ltd
Printed and bound in Great Britain by
Page Bros, Norwich, Norfolk

CONTENTS

ACKNOWLEDGEMENTS

The lines from R S Thomas' poem, 'The Presence', are reproduced fron his *Collected Poems* with the permission of the Orion Publishing Group Ltd.

Quotations from the Bible are from the *New Revised Standard Version* Bible, copyright © 1989, by the Division of Christian Education of the National Council of the Churches of Christ in the USA, and are used by permission. All rights reserved.

The author is especially grateful to David Brown and Bridget Nichols for reading the text and suggesting a number of improvements. Unfortunately, he remains responsible for this final version.

PREFACE

At the beginning of the third millennium a new mood is sweeping through the Christian churches. This mood is reflected in a more radical commitment to discipleship among a laity who wish to be theologically informed and fully equipped for Christian ministry in the secular world.

Exploring Faith: theology for life is designed for people who want to take Christian theology seriously in a way that engages the mind, involves the heart, and seeks active expression in the way we live. Those who explore their faith in this way are beginning to shape a theology for life.

Exploring Faith: theology for life is rooted in the individual experience of the world and in the ways through which God is made known in the world. Such experience is related to and interpreted in the light of the Christian tradition. Each volume is written by a scholar who has clear authority in the area of theology discussed and who takes seriously the ways in which busy adults learn. The series aims to open up key aspects of theology and explore these in dialogue with the readers' own experience.

The volumes are suitable for all those who wish to learn more about the Christian faith and ministry, including those who have already taken Christian basic courses (such as *Alpha* and *Emmaus*) and have been inspired to undertake further study, those preparing to take theology as an undergraduate course, and those already engaged on degree programmes. The volumes have been developed for individuals to work on alone or for groups to study together.

Already groups of Christians are using the *Exploring Faith: theology for life* series throughout the United Kingdom, linked by exciting credit-bearing initiatives pioneered jointly by the churches and the academy. There are a number of ways in which learning Christians can find their way into award-bearing programmes through the series *Exploring Faith: theology for life*.

The series editors wish to express their personal thanks to colleagues who have helped them shape the series identity, especially Diane Drayson, Evelyn Jackson, Susan Thomas and Virginia Hearn, and to the individual authors who have produced high quality text on schedule and so generously accepted firm editorial direction. The editorial work has been supported by the North of England Institute for Christian Education and the Welsh National Centre for Religious Education.

Leslie J Francis
Jeff Astley

INTRODUCTION

Human language is one of the greatest inventions of the human species.

Our words are an integral part of 'our world'. Not only do they give form to our experience, as we paint language onto the flickering images of our perception in order to discriminate and describe, we also rely on language in every department of life for most of our communication, learning and thinking.

It is not surprising, then, that *religious* language is the primary medium for portraying the divine, and for religious communication, religious learning and religious thinking. This book maps the contours of religious language. It surveys the variety of ways in which religious believers both speak to God and speak about God, and tries to respond to the serious criticisms that have been raised about different aspects of this 'God-talk'.

Such concerns are of signal importance to religious language *users* – those who talk to God in prayer, hear about God in sermons, read about God in Scripture and theology, and speak and think about the God in whom they believe. But they are also central to the work of those students of religion, unbelievers as well as believers, who wish to explore this central phenomenon of religion. While the focus in this text is on the Judaeo-Christian tradition, much of what is discussed here is applicable to other religious faiths.

The book begins with an overview of the variety of ways in which language is used in faith and religion. It moves on to consider the functions of language in religious experience and the religious life, particularly in prayer and worship. Two chapters are devoted to a consideration of the important area of 'descriptive' religious language, both figurative and literal. Problems relating to the meaningfulness of religious language and the interpretation of Scripture are addressed, and the pastoral and ethical significance of God-talk explored. Illustrations are drawn throughout from everyday speech as well as the Christian tradition.

After reading this book, adult learners and other students should be familiar with the range of religious language used in Scripture, worship and theology. They should be better able to resolve misunderstandings in theology and religion that are caused by an inadequate understanding of the language used about God and the language used to address God, and to tackle for themselves some of the problems that are posed for the contemporary person who speaks about her faith and her God. In these ways religious believers can be helped to become more confident in their use of religious language, and students of religion will be better able to recognise what is going on when religious people speak of God or to God.

Exploring God-Talk will prove useful for two groups: adult Christian learners working individually or on courses, and students beginning to study theology or philosophy of religion in sixth forms, colleges and universities. Much of the material in this book has its origins in courses that I have taught in all these different contexts.

1. MAPPING THE CONTOURS OF RELIGIOUS LANGUAGE

Introduction

In this book we shall explore the ways in which we and/or other people use religious language. As the story about the man who wanted to find the way to Dublin makes clear, before beginning a journey it is wise to give some thought to one's starting-point. So let us reflect on where we start from as we prepare to set out on this journey of exploration.

For many readers of this book, this will involve listening to themselves. If you are a religious language-user, how do you speak of and to God, and what do you mean by that God-talk? Other readers will be starting from a different place. Not being religious language-users themselves, they will need to listen to other people's God-talk. How do you think that *they* use religious language, and what can they possibly mean by it?

Reflecting on experience
Think about some religious language that you have recently used or heard (or read). Jot down a few significant examples of religious words, phrases or sentences that either mean a lot to you, or clearly meant a lot to the people who used them.

I hope that you were able to come up with a wide range of examples, because God-talk is very varied indeed. In this chapter we shall look around us at the variety that is displayed by the landscape of religious language, in preparation for the more detailed mapping exercise that lies ahead in this book.

The varieties of religious language

I offer below my own list of examples of religious language. It is drawn from a range of sources, including interviews, biblical texts, written prayers, hymns and liturgies, and books of contemporary theology.

EXERCISE

Look over the collection of items of God-talk that you gathered earlier, together with my list, and see if you can begin to sort the material (both the expressions and their component words) into some sort of *classification*. What categories of religious language are illustrated here? (As you may end up with more than one set of categories, any particular item could fall into two or more categories.)

(a) 'Perhaps God calmed down when he got a son.'

(b) 'God's "sempiternity" is that of boundless life, and the hope of immortality is the hope of future participation, by God's recreative act, in God's own endless future.'

(c) 'I was standing at the sink with a load of washing, when I had a vision – it was as if everything had a spirit inside, almost talking to you of the nature of it, of its essence. It was the atmosphere of "God walking in the garden in the cool of the day".'

(d) 'The Lord is near.'

(e) 'Truly the Lord is our shield,
the Holy One of Israel is our king.'

(f) 'Lord, have mercy upon us.'

(g) 'I, in my mind, think of [Jesus] still as an outer limb of God.'

(h) 'Come, Holy Ghost, our souls inspire,
And lighten with celestial fire.'

(i) 'Our soul is kindly rooted in God in endless love.'

(j) 'The grace of our Lord Jesus Christ,
the love of God
and the fellowship of the Holy Spirit
be with you all.'

(k) 'God is enriched in the world-process, and conversely draws that process towards new value by posing to it the possibilities that open in his experience.'

(l) 'The cross of Jesus is the slaying of the Logos.'
(m) 'Why did God let it happen?'
(n) 'I believe in Jesus Christ.'
(o) 'I baptise you
      in the name of the Father,
      and of the Son
      and of the Holy Spirit.'
(p) 'Mild he lays his glory by,
      Born that man no more may die,
      Born to raise the sons of earth,
      Born to give them second birth!'

There is always more than one way of slicing a cake. Not only can we produce slices of different sizes, we can also wield our knives in different planes so that the different slicings interconnect, as one process of division cuts across another. In categorising religious language in this chapter I shall employ just three, rather different, schemes of classification. You may have found others that are equally valid, and additional distinctions will become apparent as you go through this book.

Theology, religion and piety

In the title of this chapter, and throughout the book generally, I use the phrase 'religious language' in a very wide sense to cover:

• the language used in prayer, worship, Scripture and ordinary religious reflection and expression; and
• the more conceptually-developed and often technical discourse that characterises the speech and writing of academic theologians.

Others, however, do not use the phrase this widely. Many commentators label the first set of activities as 'religion', and its linguistic form as *religious language*. They distinguish this from the second category of 'theology', which is marked by *theological language*. When the cake is cut along that line, religious language is described as being most explicitly grounded in religious experience and practice. This 'language of living faith' includes *talk to God*, which is frequently personal, intense, metaphorical and autobiographical, as well as being occasional and unsystematic. 'Communion with God, symbolically focused in liturgy, is the primary locus of religious language for the Christian' (Wainwright, 1980, p. 21). By contrast, the second-order language of theology is entirely *talk about God*, and is therefore likely to be 'cooler' – more objective and impersonal. This form of discourse seeks intellectual clarification, and therefore precision and a coherent system. Paul Ricoeur describes it as 'second degree discourse', which is 'derived and subordinate' when compared with the original linguistic expression of a community of faith (Ricoeur, 1980, pp. 74, 90). Understood along these lines, theology may be said to operate by grading and sorting, classifying, appraising and systematising religious language's 'riotous mixture of phrases' (Ramsey, 1957, p. 156). Its task is that of constructing and honing concepts, belief-systems and arguments out of the rich source of religion. John Macquarrie claims that 'not all God-talk would qualify as theology, for we reserve the name for the most sophisticated and reflective ways of talking about God' (Macquarrie, 1967, p. 11).

EXERCISE

How do you respond to this distinction? Even if you want to offer some criticisms of it, look back over the list of sentences and phrases on pp. 2–3 and ask yourself which of them are best categorised as *religious* language and which as *theological* language?

Are some of the examples difficult to locate, appearing to straddle both categories?

Although this distinction is a very important one, you may be unhappy with such a sharp demarcation between religion and theology. Those who use the phrase religious language to cover *both* categories often distinguish within it between *primary* ('metaphorical') and *secondary* ('conceptual') religious language, sometimes treating theological language as some sort of specialised mixture of the two (McFague, 1983, pp. 22–33, 117). (In my list on pp. 2–3, (d) and (e) would be good examples of the primary category, and (b), (k) and (l) of the secondary category – although there are elements of metaphor there too.)

Such an account may tempt us to think of theological language as a subset of religious language: a specialised form of religious language that is particularly suited to the intellectual cut and thrust of the academy. Many definitions of theology treat it as an academic study or discipline (or, better, disciplines) – and therefore as a task that is 'appropriate to a minority of Christians, usually seen as an intellectual elite' (Sykes, 1983). Yet scholars also acknowledge a broader sense of the term that may be applied to a wider range of people (Ford, 1999, pp. 10, 15). According to Edward Farley, until the eighteenth century 'theology was not just for the scholar or teacher but was the wisdom proper to the life of the believer' (Farley, 1988, p. 88; cf. 1983, chapter 2). This wider, democratic understanding of theology treats it as a label for *reflective faith*. Understood in this way, theology is a disposition and orientation of the soul that constitutes the believer's personal, salvific (that is, saving) knowledge of God, very different from the abstract, impersonal knowledge that results from the more recondite, specialist reflection of a scholarly discipline of investigation. Farley insists that this more ordinary and everyday species of theology is a part of *every* Christian's vocation. In this sense, all Christians do theology.

What is in mind here is a form of theology that is *lay* in several senses: not only is it shared in by the whole Church, it is also the theology that typifies the non-expert. In this latter sense it may be described as *ordinary theology*. Elsewhere I have defined this type of theology as 'the theology and theologizing of Christians who have received little or no theological education of a scholarly, academic or systematic kind' (Astley, 2002, p. 56). Unlike more academic versions of theology, ordinary theology relies on aphorism, personal biography and anecdote; it is rich in story and figurative language; and it appears in 'bits and pieces' rather than as a finished, carefully argued system. *Academic theology*, by contrast, is more consistent and structured, and frequently employs carefully defined technical terms.

In distinguishing between ordinary and academic theology, however, we should recognise that the difference is one of degree – sometimes very marked degree – rather than a distinction of kind. (Both, for example, are 'reflective' forms of God-talk.) Nevertheless, ordinary theology is the category that is most readily designated as a form of religious or spiritual talk; we may describe it as a *religious* theology. Academic theology itself draws on religion, of course, for the academic theologian's work is dependent in the end on the primary world of religion (what else could it depend on?), and many academic theologians retain an ordinary theological 'core'. But ordinary theology is nearer to its religious roots, and draws much more heavily on and is more moulded by the spiritual attitudes, values, beliefs, practices and experiences that express and constitute religious faith, worship and piety.

A great deal of ordinary theology lies close to and often incorporates what might be called *celebratory* rather than *critical* theology. Theology as 'celebratory' is a category that Rowan Williams describes as characteristic of the hymnody and preaching of the Church's early centuries, as well as of 'the more intelligent modern choruses, and of contemporary Eastern Orthodox theology' (Williams, 2000a, pp. xiii–xv). This way of doing theology has also been described as 'kneeling theology' or 'theology at prayer', a form of theology that adopts a very different posture from the 'sitting theology' or 'theology at the desk' that is favoured by the academic theologian (von Balthasar, 1989, p. 208). Ordinary theology shares too some of the marks of what the novelist Ursula Le Guin has called the 'mother tongue' of the home. This is the language of communication and relationship, which she distinguishes from the distancing, arm's length objectivity and analysis of the 'father tongue' that we need to go to college fully to learn (Le Guin, 1989, pp. 147–151).

From ordinary to academic speech

It may be that if you revisit the last exercise with the distinction between ordinary theology and academic theology in mind, you will again find it hard to locate some of the expressions firmly in one category rather than the other. Attempts to make too hard and fast a distinction between the different categories must be resisted, whether between religious and theological language, or between ordinary theology and the more 'extraordinary' (academic, scientific, scholarly) type. It would not be true to say that all ordinary theology is thoroughly spiritual, experiential or 'religious', nor that every example of academic theology is irredeemably impersonal or theoretical. We should think instead of a continuous spectrum, the extremes of which are more easy to distinguish than are the intermediate or 'mixed' forms. A better, because more dynamic, analogy can be found in the pattern made by a stone when it is thrown into the middle of a large pond.

> The ripples go out from the disturbance at the centre so that, given the right conditions, they eventually change the entire surface, interacting with the pond's own contours as they spread from the point where the stone hit the water. In this analogy (or allegory), the pond represents ourselves with our thoughts and feelings, its surface is our language. Whatever we take the stone to be, the splash represents some sort of

religious experience, religious change or religious learning. The ripples that lie close to the point of the stone's impact are large disturbances, which form regular circles around it. These ripples then move out across the pond, changing as they move: their amplitude declines somewhat and they accommodate themselves more to the structure of the pond, metamorphosing from perfect circles to more irregular and sometimes interacting patterns (as they 'bounce off' rocks and other features).

Ordinary theology is like the early ripples coming out from a religious change. These represent the devotional language that arises as a direct reaction to religious experience or conversion, together with the language of personal confession, testimony and commitment . . . They are more intense, more 'moving' and more 'disturbing' than the later changes in our hearts and minds that flow from them. At the very edges of the pond the water still rises and falls in response to the experiential and learning changes at the centre, but other influences are now involved . . . These smoother, more mature, more distant and less violent perturbations at the edge will be more affected by the pond's environment and the rocks, shoals and vegetation that determine its three-dimensional shape. These ripples are the changes that represent academic theology: movements of thought and language that are more distant from the source of the original disturbance, more influenced by other factors, less particular and local, and more wide-ranging. (Astley, 2002, pp. 86–87)

I offer this analogy as a picture of the way in which ordinary theology (or primary religious language) can lead smoothly into academic theology, as the first theological agitation triggers the second. The rippling of the more conceptual and academic theology can therefore ultimately be tracked back to more everyday disturbances within the more ordinary religious language of the same person, or at least the same community. At the beginning and the end of the wave's path the differences will be very marked, as is clearly illustrated by examples (a), (c) and (g), when compared with (b) and (k), in the list on pp. 2–3 above. But at a number of intermediate points one may not be sure whether to call this linguistic ripple 'ordinary' or 'academic' theology, 'religious' or (real?) 'theological' language. (What about (h) and (i), for example, or even (m)?)

Using her own categories, Sallie McFague notes how the Nicene Creed (see below) mixes conceptual and metaphorical language (McFague,

1983, pp. 112–114). For example, the phrase 'of one Being with the Father' lies alongside the phrase 'Light from Light'. Indeed, in the creeds some words or phrases serve at one and the same time *both* as devotional, metaphorical images *and* as theological terms that carry an abstract, conceptual and highly nuanced meaning. ('Son' would be a good example of this; perhaps 'the Almighty' is another.)

Does religion mean what it says?

In the earlier classification exercise you may have distinguished some examples where language is used with its normal, 'literal' meaning from examples where the language that is applied to God, Christ or the Spirit (or the Church or Christian experience) is employed in a more figurative way. This distinction between the *metaphorical* and *literal* uses of language is of considerable significance in analysing the meaning of religious language. Most people would say that in examples (f), (j) and (l), the words 'mercy', 'love' and (most clearly) 'cross' are being used literally, with their normal meaning; whereas examples (c), (e) and (h) contain obvious metaphors ('vision', 'walking', 'shield', 'king', 'fire'). You may be unclear, however, about some of the other words, and some theologians would not agree that the words 'mercy' and 'love' can be applied literally to God.

EXERCISE

It might be useful at this stage, to study the so-called Nicene Creed, a confession of faith that was formulated in the fourth century AD and is regularly recited by Christians at the Eucharist. See if you can specify those words and phrases within this text that appear to be used (a) *literally* and (b) *metaphorically*.

Are there other words or phrases that are used with a *stretched* or *extended* meaning, but that aren't really metaphors?

(Keep a note of your conclusions from this exercise and revisit them after reading chapters 4 and 5 below.)

The Nicene Creed

(The text used here is from The English Language Liturgical Consultation, © ELLC 1988)
We believe in one God,
the Father, the Almighty,
maker of heaven and earth,
of all that is,
seen and unseen.

We believe in one Lord, Jesus Christ
the only Son of God,
eternally begotten of the Father,
God from God, Light from Light,
true God from true God,
begotten, not made,
of one Being with the Father;
through him all things were made.
For us and for our salvation he came down from heaven,
was incarnate from the Holy Spirit and the Virgin Mary
and was made man,
For our sake he was crucified under Pontius Pilate;
he suffered death and was buried.
On the third day he rose again
in accordance with the Scriptures;
he ascended into heaven
and is seated at the right hand of the Father.
He will come again in glory to judge the living and the dead,
and his kingdom will have no end.

We believe in the Holy Spirit,
the Lord, the giver of life,
who proceeds from the Father and the Son,
who with the Father and the Son is worshipped and glorified,
who has spoken through the prophets.
We believe in one holy catholic and apostolic Church.
We acknowledge one baptism for the forgiveness of sins.
We look for the resurrection of the dead,
and the life of the world to come.
Amen.

What use is religious language?

A third way of cutting the cake of religious language is to look at the different activities that people are engaged in when they speak or write religious language.

EXERCISE

Look one last time at the list on pp. 2–3 (augmented by your own list). What sort of different things are people *doing* when they talk in these ways?

I have already distinguished between talking *about* (or of) God and talking *to* God. Talking to God is found in prayer, which takes many forms: (f) and (h) are two examples in my list. Examples (a) and (b), despite their very real differences from each other, are both examples of talk about God. But some examples of religious language are not really talking about God, but doing something different: (m) asks a question; in the right circumstances (including using water in a certain way), (o) enacts a baptism. Religious language can do a lot more than just address or describe God.

We shall explore the different uses of religious language in more detail in chapters 7 and 8.

Further reading

Astley, J (2002), *Ordinary Theology: looking, listening and learning in theology*, Aldershot, Ashgate, chapter 3.

Caird, G B (1980), *The Language and Imagery of the Bible*, London, Duckworth, chapter 1.

Ford, D F (1999), *Theology: a very short introduction*, Oxford, Oxford University Press.

Macquarrie, J (1967), *God-Talk: an examination of the language and logic of theology*, London, SCM.

McFague, S (1982), *Metaphorical Theology: models of God in religious language*, London, SCM.

2. RELIGIOUS LANGUAGE AND RELIGIOUS EXPERIENCE

Introduction

There is an intimate relationship between the experiences that we all have as human beings, and the language that we all use.

Many assume that our language evolved as a dramatic refinement of the vocalisations and non-verbal displays, gestures and rituals of our human and non-human ancestors (see Pinker, 1994, chapter 11; Dunbar, 1996). Its purpose, presumably, was to communicate to others something about our 'objective' sense experiences of the outside world, on the one hand, and our inner, 'subjective' experiences of our basic feeling states and more complex emotions, on the other. Language is still our most effective tool for 'expressing', 'conveying' or 'communicating' human experience. Of course it does much more than this. In particular, it is the medium of conceptualisation, reasoning and imagination – or, as Thomas Carlyle has it, 'the flesh-garment, the body, of thought' (*Sartor Resartus*, 1834). But the relationship between our thoughts or ideas and our language seems much closer than the relationship between our language and the 'other world' of experience.

Many writers have complained about language's inadequacy to its task of expressing and communicating. The novelist Gustave Flaubert famously wrote in *Madame Bovary* (1857) that 'human speech is like a cracked kettle on which we tap crude rhythms for bears to dance to, while we long to make music that will melt the stars'. Such failures are particularly evident when we seek to express and communicate our experiences.

Reflecting on experience
Think of some circumstances in which you have said or felt that 'language fails me'. How might language's ability to express and communicate be improved?

We tend to admire others who have a better facility with language than we have ourselves. When I get into a linguistic muddle with an argument or exposition, I envy a colleague who is more precise and lucid in his presentations. When I try to recount an amusing incident, I envy my friend who has such an entrancing yet natural way of telling stories about herself. When looking at a landscape or work of art, I envy those writers who can capture visual experience in words in a way that not only expresses what I see, but helps me to see it differently and in a much richer way. When I listen to music that moves me greatly, or taste wine that delights me, I envy those experts who always seem to find the right words to describe such experiences. Most of all, perhaps, I envy the poet who knows how to express the human experiences that we all share, so that I respond, 'That's it. That's what it feels like. That is the experience I live through.'

It is not only that all these people possess, whereas I patently lack, some additional knowledge or talent, or even just a wider vocabulary. I believe that the main difference between us is that they are more *practised* in their use of language. (I don't doubt that they are more talented and sensitive, articulate or clever as well, but there is little I can do to bridge those gaps.) I suspect that when words fail me, it is largely because I have not worked hard enough or long enough or often enough at my language so that my words can succeed better. If I were to try to speak more, or even write more, about my experiences – whether 'out there' (experiences of the world and other people) or 'in here' (my emotions and feelings) – my words would fail less often, and less completely. Practice does not always make perfect, but it nearly always makes us *better* at doing something.

Human language and religious experience

Should we adopt the same diagnosis with regard to religion? Two things need to be said. First, that language can never wholly capture the heart of religion; but, second, that we need to *keep on talking*.

EXERCISE

Reflect on the possible reasons why religious discourse might prove, in the end, to be inadequate.

Why, then, should people bother to keep on with their God-talk?

If the content of our sense experience of the sensible (that is, visible, audible and tangible) world is often so difficult to put into words, we should not expect religious language to do a better job for religious experience. God is necessarily a mystery that transcends – goes beyond, exceeds – our experience and our language. God is said to be radically different, radically other: God is the unlimited creator Spirit, infinite in power and utterly boundless in love. According to Pseudo-Dionysius, a theologian who flourished around AD 500, 'the inscrutable One is out of reach of every rational process. Nor can any words come up to the inexpressible Good, this One, this Source of all unity, this supra-existent Being' (*The Divine Names*). As we shall see in the following chapters, because our ordinary language has developed in order to allow us to talk about what is finite and limited – ordinary things and ordinary people, it must be stretched almost to breaking point in order to become sufficiently big enough, and different enough, to approximate to a representation of God. The object of religious experience surely *must* exceed our religious language.

> We receive this mystical knowledge of God clothed in none of the kinds of images, in none of the sensible representations, which our mind makes use of in other circumstances. Accordingly in this knowledge, since the senses and the imagination are not employed, we get neither form nor impression, nor can we give any account or furnish any likeness, although the mysterious and sweet-tasting wisdom comes home so clearly to the inmost parts of our soul. Fancy a man seeing a certain kind of thing for the first time in his life. He can understand it, use and enjoy it, but he cannot apply a name to it, nor communicate any idea of it, even though all the while it be a mere thing of sense. How much greater will be his powerlessness when it goes beyond the senses! This is the peculiarity of the divine language. The more infused, intimate, spiritual, and super-sensible it is, the more does it exceed the senses, both inner and outer, and impose silence upon them. (St John of the Cross, *The Dark Night of the Soul*, quoted in James, 1960, p. 393)

> Moreover, something is or seems,
> That touches me with mystic gleams,
> Like glimpses of forgotten dreams –

> Of something felt, like something here;
> Of something done, I know not where;

Such as no language may declare.
('The Two Voices', Tennyson, 1916, p. 35)

In many situations it is the nature of the experience itself that transcends language, straining the descriptive resources of the person undergoing the experience. Even religious emotion, including the 'longing' and 'yearning' of the soul for God, can 'far outpass the power of human telling', as the fifteenth-century hymn reminds us. Early on in his great work *The Idea of the Holy*, Rudolf Otto writes that whoever cannot direct their mind to a moment of deeply felt religious experience, 'is requested to read no further' (Otto, 1925, p. 8). He believed that it was futile to discuss religious experience with people who had never had such an experience.

But many who have known the most extreme forms of religious experience *have* attempted to convey some sense of it in human words (even St John of the Cross). In 'describing human experiences which few have had and for which, consequently, there is no established set of literal terms', mystics and others appeal to metaphors in order to find words adequate to the experience. So they speak of such things as 'the dark night of the soul', 'the spiritual marriage', or of entering 'the cloud of unknowing' (Soskice, 1985, pp. 96, 151). This figurative language is often very striking. In giving an account of the 'prayer of quiet' in *The Way of Perfection*, St Teresa of Avila writes that the soul is 'like a babe at the breast of its mother', who feeds it without its having to move its own lips. Elsewhere she writes that her experiences transcend both understanding and precise description: 'Anyone who has experienced this will to some extent understand. It cannot be expressed more clearly, since all that happens is so obscure' (*The Interior Castle*).

St Augustine famously claimed that even the one who has most to say about God is, in effect, dumb; and that doctrines and creeds can do no more than 'fence a mystery'. At least in speaking of the Trinity, 'human language labours under an altogether great poverty'. The only alternative is to remain silent, however, and that is unacceptable; we have to do the best we can, for we must say *something*. Yet centuries later, St Thomas Aquinas gave up writing his massive treatise, the *Summa Theologiae*, after having received a profound religious experience while saying Mass. 'All I have written', he explained, 'seems like straw.'

But Immanuel Kant rebuked those who entirely give up on language as a medium for expression by comparing them with a flying bird that imagines its flight would be easier in empty space. For humans, there is no alternative to the medium of language. It is perhaps too obvious to say that *we* would know less, not more, about God if all those who claim to have had any experience of God chose inarticulate silence as their only response. Further, whatever contact God had with the prophet, 'it was by way of language and the images and meanings and insights it generates' (Barrett, 1990, p. 219). Some contend that if we strip language away from religious experience we shall be left with very little, if anything (but cf. Davis, 1989, chapter 6).

Taking a more radical line, it has been said that the function of at least some mystical expressions is not to describe reality at all, but 'to evoke the knowledge of *how* to live freely' and 'to recondition the expectations about the subjective factors in one's experience' (Streng, 1978, pp. 153–154; see also Miles, 1972). The radical Christian theologian Don Cupitt interprets these supposed 'experiences' as 'the product of a process of unconscious religious thought' which merely say 'something important and interesting about *the experient*' (Cupitt, 2001, p. 79).

> The mystics do not offer us descriptions of language-transcending experiences. If we look at any canonical list of mystics, what one notices straightaway is that these people are writers, wordsmiths. Not reporters but writers, . . . who convey their message, not by pointing to something outside language, but by the way they play games with language . . . What they write is best interpreted as a slightly mocking and subversive commentary upon the officially approved forms of words for speaking about God. (Cupitt, 1998, p. 61)

Focusing on religious experience

But let us return to more traditional interpretations. An *experience* is essentially something that we 'live through' or 'undergo'. It happens to us, producing changes in cognition (belief) and affect (feeling). Religious experience has been defined as 'a state of mind or feeling induced by factors beyond ordinary explanation' (Dillistone, 1983, p. 205).

As we have seen, the phrase 'religious experience', like the general use of the word 'experience', is ambiguous. It may refer to 'subjective' feeling states of longing, guilt, acceptance, worth, justification, election, joy, and so on. This usage parallels such claims as 'I feel elated/ depressed' or 'I experience elation/depression'. On the other hand, the phrase may denote an 'objective' experience of a religious reality: in the Christian case, a supposed experience of the presence or activity of God, the risen Christ or the Holy Spirit. The analogy here is to the claim that 'I feel the table' or 'I experience the light'. Many surveys of the psychology or phenomenology of religious experience cover both forms of experience. Because philosophers of religion are concerned with the epistemology of religion (the theory of religious knowledge), they focus primarily on those religious experiences that are claimed to be of 'cognitive significance' ('cognitive' being understood here in the sense of 'factual' or 'truth-claiming'). These experiences are usually described as *experiences of* some supernatural entity. They are often explicitly distinguished from subjective religious experiences such as states of felt confidence or dependence. While the existence of God may be thought to be the best explanation for the existence of these religious emotions, many would deny that they are direct experiences of God.

Friedrich Schleiermacher (1768–1834) has been described as the first 'important thinker in the Christian tradition who shifted attention from text and doctrine to religious experience' (Smart and Konstantine, 1991, p. 133), although we should note that the contemplative and mystical traditions had for centuries laid great stress on personal experience in religion. In viewing Christianity as a particular stream of religious consciousness in history, Schleiermacher was reacting against the interpretations of religion favoured by the eighteenth-century Enlightenment or 'Age of Reason'. He argued that religion was neither a form of knowing nor a form of doing, but something distinctive – a matter of *piety*.

For Schleiermacher, religion as piety was essentially a feeling or intuition, not a form of reasoning. He variously described it as 'a sense and taste for the infinite', 'a feeling of absolute dependence' and as 'God-consciousness'. 'To feel oneself absolutely dependent and to be conscious of being in relation with God are one and the same thing . . . . God is given to us in feeling in an original way' (1928, p. 17). Schleiermacher was the standard-bearer for all those who criticise objective, dispassionate doctrine in the name of personal, felt religion.

> No man is pious, however perfectly he understands these principles and conceptions, however much he possesses them in clearest consciousness, who cannot show that they have originated in himself and, being the outcome of his own feeling, are peculiar to himself. (Schleiermacher, 1958, p. 47)

In Schleiermacher's view, *doctrines* were secondary and derivative: mere shadows of the religious emotions. They originate in religion but lie at one remove from it, being the result of 'contemplation of feeling, . . . reflection and comparison'. As 'general expressions for definite feelings', doctrines are not necessary for religion itself, 'scarcely even for communicating religion, but reflection requires and creates them' (1958, p. 87). Christian doctrines, Schleiermacher declared, are 'accounts of the Christian religious affections set forth in speech' (Schleiermacher, 1928, p. 76). God is *directly* known only in religious experience.

Schleiermacher's approach to Christian theology has been called a 'theology from below up' or the 'subjective method' of doing theology. As such, it has been widely censured as a matter of finding out about God by human introspection rather than by listening to God, and therefore as an anthropocentric theology or psychologising of revelation. Karl Barth wrote:

> the Reformers propagated the teaching of the Word of God in its correlation with faith as the work of the Holy Spirit in man.
> Schleiermacher reversed the order of this thought. What interests him is the question of man's action in regard to God. (Barth, 1972, p. 459)

Schleiermacher's work is often presented as part of a 'Romanticist' reaction to the arid intellectualism and moralism of the eighteenth-century Enlightenment, and much of his language can be criticised as being concerned only with subjective feeling from which God would have to be inferred (Rudolf Otto, who was much influenced by Schleiermacher, interpreted him in this way). But his intention appears rather to have been to speak of an objective *apprehension* or emotional *perception* of the spiritual.

Forms of religious experience

Religious experience can take many forms, from interpreting everyday events as examples of God's providence, to powerful experiences of God through meditation or worship. 'Visions' or 'auditions', in which a divine figure is 'seen' or 'heard', are very much rarer, and I shall not deal with them here. Two classic modes of religious experience are the *numinous* and the *mystical*.

In a numinous experience, God is known in an 'outer' experience, as a holy presence, a transcendent 'Wholly Other' reality over against the person who undergoes the experience. Mystical experiences, by contrast, are 'inner' experiences of the soul's union or identity with the immanent God – that is, with a God who is intimately involved with creation, including persons. Interestingly, the metaphorical language that is used to describe these different aspects of God points in two opposite directions. Thus the transcendence (otherness, difference) of God is expressed in terms of God's being 'far off', 'beyond' or 'above', whereas the spatial metaphors of immanence speak of a God who is 'close' to us, even 'within' us.

This spatial language is, of course, used quite generally in religion. A frequently cited test for whether people really believe that all religious language is to be taken literally is whether they think of God as residing, in the words of an old children's hymn, 'above the bright blue sky'.

EXERCISE

Study a hymn book or Bible concordance, looking for metaphors of: (a) height and depth, and (b) distance and presence. Do these metaphors still serve to express authentic religious experience and religious reflection?

In your view, how are God's transcendence and immanence best symbolised outside language – for example, in church architecture, decoration and furnishing?

Awful presence

The terminology of the 'numinous' experience of the holy, a form of cognition that he claims 'does not rely on the evidence of the senses', was coined by Rudolf Otto. Otto's account of the experience is striking and has been very widely praised. As we have seen, he argues that it is something that we need to have experienced ourselves in order to understand, although he does allow that there are secular analogies to it.

EXERCISE
📖 **Read Isaiah 6:1–8; Mark 9:2–8.**

Note in these famous passages the relation between human language and religious experience at two levels:

(a) in the verbal responses made by the prophet or disciple;

(b) in the account of the setting and the overall experience.

Otto's analysis offers a powerful portrayal of such overwhelming religious experiences, which he assumes to be irreducible to any other mental state and treats as the foundation of all religion. The numinous experience has two components:
- a creaturely feeling of dependence and nothingness; and
- a sense of the presence of an overwhelming being.

It combines the apparently opposing elements of dread and fascination in the experience of a transcendent 'Other', which Otto designates the *mysterium tremendum et fascinans* – the daunting yet alluring mystery. Notice the vivid language he employs to capture this experience of the holy.

> Let us consider the deepest and most fundamental element in all strong and sincerely felt religious emotion . . . we are dealing with something for which there is only one appropriate expression, *mysterium tremendum*. The feeling of it may at times come sweeping like a gentle tide, pervading the mind with a tranquil mood of deepest worship. It may pass over into a more set and lasting attitude of the soul, continuing, as it were, thrillingly vibrant and resonant, until at last it dies away and the soul resumes its 'profane', non-religious mood of everyday experience. It may burst in sudden eruption up from the depths of the soul with spasms and convulsions, or lead to the strangest excitements, to intoxicated frenzy, to transport, and to ecstasy. It has its wild and demonic forms and can sink to an almost grisly horror and shuddering. It has its crude, barbaric antecedents and early manifestations, and again it may be developed into something beautiful and pure and glorious. It may become the hushed, trembling, and speechless humility of the creature in the presence of –

whom or what? In the presence of that which is a *Mystery* inexpressible and above all creatures. . . .

The qualitative *content* of the numinous experience, to which 'the mysterious' stands as *form*, is in one of its aspects the element of daunting 'awefulness' [*sic*] and 'majesty', . . . but it is clear that it has at the same time another aspect, in which it shows itself as something uniquely attractive and *fascinating*. . . . The daemonic-divine object may appear to the mind an object of horror and dread, but at the same time it is no less something that allures with a potent charm, and the creature, who trembles before it, utterly cowed and cast down, has always at the same time the impulse to turn to it, nay even to make it somehow his own. The 'mystery' is for him not merely something to be wondered at but something that entrances him; and beside that in it which bewilders and confounds, he feels a something that captivates and transports him with a strange ravishment, rising often enough to the pitch of dizzy intoxication . . . (Otto, 1925, pp. 12–13, 31)

According to Otto, this numinous experience is non-rational and non-moral. But God-talk needs somehow to represent both the experience and its object. Otto claims that rational theology and moral characterisations of God arise subsequent to the experience as *ideograms*: that is, analogies that are applied to God on the basis of analogous human experiences. For example, our experience of fear, which is analogous to religious dread in the face of the holy, leads us to speak of God as 'wrathful'.

Intimate union

Mystical experience gives rise to equally powerful and intriguing forms of religious language; like numinous experiences these are experienced quite widely at various levels of intensity (Robinson, 1977; Hardy, 1979; Hay, 1982). Scholars distinguish *introvertive mystics* who deliberately shut off their senses, plunging into the depths of their own selves to be united with God, from *extrovertive mystics* (or 'Nature mystics') who utilise their physical senses (Stace, 1960, p. 61). The different types employ different linguistic imagery. In Christian mysticism, even though 'the soul feels itself to be united with God by love', the mystic's individual ego is not annihilated by nor wholly identified with God, only transformed and 'deified'. An appropriate analogy here – hinted at by some of the mystics themselves – is that of a close sexual union, with the soul being 'enveloped' or 'penetrated' by God (Zaehner, 1957, pp. 29, 150–152). But mystics employ a whole dictionary of imagery:

> The Lord takes up this small bird and puts it into the nest where it may be quiet. He has watched it fluttering for a long time, trying with its understanding and its will and all its strength to find God and please Him; and now He is pleased to give it its reward in this life. . . .

> I was wondering when I decided to write this . . . how the soul is occupied at that time. Then the Lord said to me: 'It dissolves utterly, my daughter, to rest more and more in Me. It is no longer itself that lives; it is I.' . . .

> I can only say that the soul conceives itself to be near God . . .

> (St Teresa of Avila, *The Interior Castle*, quoted in Happold, 1970, pp. 352–354)

Nevertheless, this language of direct intimate contact with God should be contrasted with claims of a *total* identification with God or absorption into God, which are much more common in Eastern religions. These latter experiences are even more difficult to describe; because they are said to transcend the duality of the subject-object distinction. 'Experience' may not even be an appropriate word.

EXERCISE

Do you recognise any elements in these descriptions of numinous or mystical awareness that chime in with your own experience, or that of other people you know?

Can you think of hymns, Bible passages or pieces of religious poetry or prose that succeed in expressing similar experiences?

Talking about revelation

Revelation is often treated as the radical alternative to religious experience – a divinely originating knowledge of God 'from above', rather than a human phenomenon seeking God 'from below'. But it is better to think of the two as complementary: in order for there to be any revelation, God must do something *and* human beings must experience this 'unveiling'. 'To disclose oneself one has to make oneself apparent. . . . at the heart of revelation there lies religious experience' (Smart, 1969, p. 119); 'Every intuition and every original feeling proceeds from revelation' (Schleiermacher, 1958, p. 89).

Two widely held understandings adopt different views of the status of the language associated with revelation. On the *propositional* view, God reveals propositions about Godself; on the *non-propositional* view, God reveals Godself and it is up to humans to render their interpretations of these experiences into language.

	Propositional View	**Non-Propositional View**
Content of revelation:	divinely-authenticated *truths* about God	*God* acting in history
Nature of faith:	an obedient acceptance of these revealed truths	a human awareness of God and God's activity disclosed through the world
Status of Scripture and tradition:	(often) regarded as an infallible record of divine truths, but this may be subject to error through human sin and fallibility	regarded as a fallible witness to or record of human religious experience, particularly of God acting in history
Status of theology:	frequently understood as either *natural* (can be worked out by unaided human reason), or supernaturally *revealed* (as here)	*all* theology is understood as human interpretation of God's revelation in history, known through religious experience

These two interpretations of revelation seem to imply two different underlying analogies.

- Propositional revelation best fits an *auditory model*, in which God 'speaks' the 'word of the Lord' and humans 'hear' and remember God's self-revelation – a divine message that they then have to interpret and record.
- Non-propositional revelation seems to imply, by contrast, a *visual model*, in which humans 'see' God's 'acts' (in history, Nature and Jesus) and then describe, interpret and record these events, together

with what they infer from them about God's character and intentions.

EXERCISE
Which of these two interpretations:
(a) is closer to the biblical understanding;
(b) is more defensible?

The non-propositional view seems to be a plausible account of how historical events are interpreted as revelatory by the authors of Scripture. Encounter theologians, such as Barth, adopt a similar position; it is mainly represented, however, by liberal scholars who argue that: "'God speaking" is a myth for "the development of human insights in response to Divine guidance"' (Ward, 1994, p. 129). (See Chapter 3 below.)

Prophetic religious experience, on the other hand, would seem to suggest a propositional analysis. This is often disparaged as a type of 'divine dictation theory', in which God ensures that his words are infallibly recorded in Scripture. However, there is no need to insist that the divine words that enter the minds of the human recipients of revelation (possibly through some form of telepathic communication) are received, understood or recorded by them without any errors creeping in.

Further reading

Cupitt, D (1998), *Mysticism after Modernity*, Oxford, Blackwell.

Dulles, A (1983), *Models of Revelation*, Dublin, Gill and Macmillan.

Happold, F C (1970), *Mysticism: a study and an anthology*, Harmondsworth, Penguin.

Hardy, A (1979), *The Spiritual Nature of Man: a study of contemporary religious experience*, Oxford, Oxford University Press.

Hay, D (1982), *Exploring Inner Space: scientists and religious experience*, Harmondsworth, Penguin.

Hick, J (1990), *Philosophy of Religion*, Englewood Cliffs, New Jersey, Prentice-Hall, chapter 5.

Hood, R W (ed.) (1995), *Handbook of Religious Experience*, Birmingham, Alabama, Religious Education Press.

James, W (1960), *The Varieties of Religious Experience*, London, Collins.

Ward, K (1994), *Religion and Revelation: a theology of revelation in the world's religions*, Oxford, Oxford University Press, pp. 209–232.

3. TALKING TO GOD AND LISTENING TO GOD

Introduction

Much of the most distinctive religious language is to be found when people address God in religious vows or other expressions of commitment, and engage in religious speech in the context of prayer and worship. This is God-talk as talking to God. 'The language of worship begins with the vocative' (Smart, 1972, p. 11). But what is meant by talking to God?

And does God talk back? The prophetic books of the Hebrew Bible are punctuated by phrases of divine endorsement, placed there to encourage the reader to treat the prophet's words as God-talk in the most radical sense of that phrase: 'The word of the LORD came to me', 'Hear the word of the LORD', 'Thus says the LORD.' Other speakers and writers have made similar claims about their own words, including some today; and in the worship of the Church readings from Scripture are often greeted with the liturgical response, 'This is the word of the Lord.' And, of course, it is commonplace for Christians to speak of the Bible as the 'word of God'.

Reflecting on experience

What do you think people mean, and what might you mean, by describing the Bible as the 'word of God'?

What do you think they mean, and what might you mean, by claiming that in prayer a person 'talks to God'?

The language of prayer and worship

Rowan Williams writes of 'the significance of prayer for an honest theology', arguing that 'speaking of God is speaking to God and opening our speech to God's; and it is speaking *of* those who have spoken to God' (Williams, 2000a, pp. 13, 8). According to Williams, religious discourse must 'articulate and confront its own temptations, its own falsehoods', in particular the extent to which 'theology has worked and continues to work in the interests of this or that system of power'. Prayer is key here. He argues that surrendering our language to God, 'articulating its own incompleteness before God', lies at the heart of religious prayer and worship. Those who engage in these most funda- mental of all religious activities acknowledge the supreme value ('worth-ship') of something beyond themselves, and their dependence on its resources. They give themselves to God, and with themselves they give their language.

Adoration and praise

These forms of prayer are pre-eminent among the categories of religious language. One secular, partial parallel is to be found in the attitudes associated with true love, which involves as a bare minimum the realisa- tion that there exists something beyond ourselves and our own concerns, beyond what Iris Murdoch called the 'fat, relentless ego' (Murdoch, 1970, p. 52). Love of God, expressed in adoration and praise, takes this process further. Worship helps us to transcend ourselves, 'going beyond' our own concerns to acknowledge another of supreme, indeed infinite worth. According to Evelyn Underhill, worship is 'an avenue which leads the creature from his inveterate self-occupation to a knowledge of God, and ultimately to that union with God which is the beatitude of the soul' (Underhill, 1936, pp. 17–18).

Murdoch also appeals to our experience of attending to or contem- plating the beauty of Nature, viewing this as an occasion for 'unselfing'. She writes:

> I am looking out of my window in an anxious and resentful state of mind, oblivious to my surroundings, brooding perhaps on some damage done to my prestige. Then suddenly I observe a hovering kestrel. In a moment everything is altered. The brooding self with its hurt vanity has disappeared. There is nothing now but kestrel. And when I return to thinking of the other matter it seems less important. (Murdoch, 1970, p. 84)

As we succumb to such a moment, 'we take a self-forgetful pleasure in the sheer alien pointless independent existence' of Nature. The world will indeed seem irrational and 'pointless' when viewed from the perspective of *my* 'point', my reasons for living. But, then, Nature isn't there simply *for me*.

EXERCISE
📖 **Read Job 38:1 to 42:6.**

(If you do not know the Book of Job, dip into the earlier chapters as well to get a taste of Job's courage and defiance in his suffering.)

What sort of an answer to Job's 'problem of suffering' does God deliver?

In this great poem, a broken human being cries out to God in his suffering and bereavement, seeking explanation, justice and consolation. But the only answer comes in a whirlwind and appears to demand that Job contemplate the otherness and arbitrariness of the creation. Is there a parallel here with Murdoch's kestrel? It would appear that the Bible also appeals to the otherness of Nature, in this context so as to evoke a sense of worship.

Many forms of religious language are available to the religious believer, including the discursive, rational, argumentative language of theological discussion. The language of true worship, however, cuts across and silences them all. True religious talk always ends up in worship. But praise is not without cost. Rowan Williams insists that praise is never simply a matter of 'euphoric fluency', nor the expression of positive religious emotion, because the novelty and otherness of God's action includes a recognition of the loss of our own self-seeking self. It is for this reason that Christian baptism is spoken of as a sharing in the death of Christ (Romans 6:3–11; Colossians 2:8–15). The cost to the worshipper is the loss of the cosy God who is just the product of human fantasies, spun out of self-concern; the 'cost' to God is the cost of human restoration (symbolised in the eucharistic breaking of the bread).

> Bible and liturgy use the metaphor of the 'sacrifice of praise'; as if the language of ascribing worth, beauty and desirability to God represented some sort of *cost* to us. So it does: praise is nothing if not the struggle to voice how the directedness of my regard depends on, is moulded by, something irreducibly other than itself. It is my speech

seeking to transmute into its own substance something on whose radical difference that very substance depends; so that it must on no account *absorb* it into itself, as that would be to lose the object's generative power. The transmutation is a reforming of the language, not the disappearance of the praised object into existing patterns of words, foreordained responses. (Williams, 2000a, p. 9)

The 'pre-existing human idiom' is thus extended and stretched – even broken – in an attempt to speak of what is beyond human understanding and human value. There is a cost, then, to religious fluency.

This breaking of language displays itself in its most extreme form in *glossolalia* or 'speaking in tongues'. This phenomenon has been described as a 'non language': spontaneous, private, preconceptual and ineffable utterances that are of the spirit rather than the intellect (Laurentin, 1977, pp. 80–82; cf. Cartledge, 2002). It is a form of speech that lies at the limit of religious language. But even within these limits, we should not expect the language of adoration and praise to be too smooth or articulate. It serves its purpose best when its words point beyond themselves, often as a consequence of repetition, or of the dissonance that comes through the employment of powerful contrasting imagery.

Thanksgiving

Whereas adoration is celebrating God solely for what God is, thanksgiving is celebrating God for what God does. Unlike the forms of prayer discussed above, the language of prayers of thanksgiving (and of supplication and confession) has a human and worldly focus as well as a divine one, in that *we* thank God for some*thing*. This mix of 'sacred' and 'secular' language – of 'heavenly Lord' with 'Uncle John's operation' – gives these prayers a very different taste.

The plain literal language that best describes both the event for which thanks are given and the human condition of gratitude is brought together in the prayer with the analogies and metaphors that are used of God. In this way the pray-er (that is, the one who prays – a word that is properly but ambiguously spelled 'prayer') generates new insights for himself and others, so that the heavenly Lord is now seen as less distant from Uncle John's release from pain. Psychologically and spiritually, each will seem relevant to the other just because they are both spoken of in the same sentence, even the same breath.

However, the doctrines of creation and providence, and the problem of suffering, raise some special difficulties for prayers of thanksgiving.

EXERCISE
📖 Read Job 2:1–10 and 'Eucharistic Prayer' A or C in
Common Worship (or the *Book of Common Prayer*'s
introduction to the Prayer of Consecration).

What can it mean to give thanks to God 'at all times and in
all places'?

These are deep waters, but Job (the early, 'patient' Job that is) and the liturgy agree in allowing the possibility of thanking God for all things, in the sense of accepting all things as a gift and of expressing (and *accepting*) one's dependence on God. The language of prayers of thanksgiving often acknowledges this wider reference, even when their main focus is on something as specific as Uncle John's operation. For example, in the service of 'Thanksgiving for the Gift of a Child' in *Common Worship* (pp. 339–343), although the introduction reads, 'We are here today to give thanks for these children', the first thanksgiving prayer thanks God for 'the wonder of new life' and 'the mystery of human love'; all who support and sustain the beginning of life; God's knowledge and love; and Jesus Christ and the salvation he brings.

Petition and intercession
'Asking God for things' (which is described generally as 'supplication' or 'impetration') includes prayer for ourselves (petition) and prayer for others (intercession). A great deal has been written on this very difficult area from a theological perspective. The language of the prayers themselves may reflect this debate, with some praying fervently for God's miraculous intervention to heal the sick, while others carefully articulate the more restricted request that God may strengthen the sufferer's courage and hope, or the doctor's skill. At its best, however, the prayer of asking is an honest expression of the pray-er's needs and concerns. To this extent, prayer *is* like talking to another person, for we often talk (although men less often than women, as we shall note in Chapter 10) just to express how we feel, rather than to get things done. How can I not speak about Uncle John's operation and my hopes for how it will turn out?

> EXERCISE
> 📖 Read the Lord's Prayer (Matthew 6:7–15; Luke 11:2–14).
>
> In what senses can this be called a 'model prayer'?

The prayer certainly includes petition, but the language places it in the context of prayer for the coming of the Kingdom and the universalising of the will of God. It may be noted that in this prayer, unlike many we hear today, this element comes *before* the particular petitions, rather than sounding like an afterthought.

Confession

In prayers of confession and repentance linguistic dissonance is particularly marked, as words are used both to invoke the holy God and to describe and confess human imperfection. Unlike confession within personal relationships, confession before God does not carry the implication that the pray-er is giving God knowledge that God did not have before, nor that he or she is seeking something (forgiveness) that is not already being offered. The words of prayer should reflect this situation. Confession also functions as a further expression of dependence on God, and its language should also be shaped so as to express the moral seriousness of one's own behaviour, but in a way that expresses hope rather than despair.

Liturgical language

David Frost contends that, in writing language for worship, the author 'must be given freedom to write as a good modern poet might write' (Frost, 1973, p. 9). Poetry is a 'way of saying' that is marked by rhythm (the repetition in time of a perceptible pattern), rhyme and the use of metaphorical language. It has been argued that all three are natural ways of expressing ourselves. (We shall look more closely at metaphor in the next chapter.)

> Rhythm is a principle of all life and all activity and is, of course, deeply involved in the experience of, and the expression of, emotion. We all know how the expressions, verbal or other, of love, hate, pain, joy, or

grief tend to fall into rhythmic patterns; the very origin of language involves rhythm. This is not to say, of course, that poetry is merely a direct expression of emotion or that the only function of rhythm in poetry is to express emotion. But it is to say that emotional expression is an essential element of poetry, that rhythm is a natural and not an artificial aspect of poetry and is, therefore, an indication of the relation of poetry to the common experience of life.

Rhyme, too, has a direct connection with our human constitution. It is related, as is rhythm, to the very origins of language, as we sense when we observe babies in their cribs playing delightedly with sounds. This 'lalling,' as it is termed, gives babies a certain satisfaction; they are acting on a pleasurable impulse. (Brooks and Warren, 1976, p. 2)

So poetry may be thought of as a natural way for religious people to express themselves in worship, rather than as something artificial and recondite (Avis, 1999, chapter 8). Furthermore, like poetry, liturgical language must be 'such that minister and people can return . . . again and again and discover further meanings at each repetition: it must have rhythm, imagery, and verbal punch'. 'The alternative to liturgical poetry', Frost claims, 'is to go back to dry, unevocative platitudes' (Frost, 1973, pp. 9, 23).

EXERCISE
Do you agree that liturgy should be treated as a form of poetry?

To illustrate his point, Frost sets side by side two alternative endings to a confession (both are now to be found in *Common Worship*). Which do you prefer as a piece of liturgical language, and why?

A	B
. . . and lead us out from darkness, to walk as children of light.	. . . and grant that we may serve you in newness of life to the glory of your name.
Amen	Amen

The odd language of prayer

In prayer, our language must always be appropriate to its task. Thinking about the language of prayer should help pray-ers to think more deeply about what they are doing when they pray. Gareth Moore, in his brilliant but disturbing essay *Believing in God* (1988), challenges us to take seriously the odd nature of prayer (and, by extension, of worship). He insists that talking to God is not like talking to Charlie or Bill. 'If I talk to God, I am not talking to people; if I am talking to people, I am not at the same time talking to God' (p. 185). Using the fiction of Otto, some-one who knows nothing at all about Christianity or any religion, but observes how religious people act and speak, Moore remarks:

> What Otto sees when he sees people talking to God (that is part of how he learns what it is to talk to God, how he learns the use of the words 'talk to God', 'pray') is that they are talking but there is nobody there they are talking to . . .
> Prayer is talking to 'the one I am with when I am with *nobody*'.

> (Moore, 1988, pp. 186, 190)

Nevertheless, Moore argues, it is part of the concept of prayer that God is always present when you pray, always there to be talked to (but not to be seen or bumped into, like Charlie) and always attentive (I do not have to attract his attention, and God doesn't get bored). God knows already what we need and want; God will not grant our requests unless they are for the good of ourselves and others, and so on. So 'there is behaviour characteristic of talking to God, but it is not the behaviour characteristic of talking to somebody'; 'asking God for something . . . is quite unlike asking somebody for something, even though similar forms of words may be used' (pp. 194, 199). All these are aspects of the 'logic' or the meaning of prayer, and they make the language of prayer – which at first sight can seem very similar to language addressed to other people – highly distinctive.

Ian Ramsey held that one fundamental element in the odd language of prayer, as of all religious language, is its *evocative role*. The narratives, poems and other linguistic forms in Scripture, prayer or hymnody, and even in technical theology, serve to evoke religious experience ('discern-ment') and revelation ('disclosure'), in addition to their task of representing the nature of the divine. The words of prayer, in particular, are used to take us into a moment of vision, a moment of silence where God discloses himself, and in God's presence we then articulate our thoughts about the world and about ourselves. (Ramsey, 1971b, p. 21)

Ramsey puts his finger here on an important feature of religious language, which is often described as 'opening people up' to religious insight or experience, or 'putting them in the right position' to receive God's revelation. It is a significant feature of the language of prayer.

Although this is very plausible as a general description of one of the functions of religious language, Ramsey's particular examples often appear rather strained (Ramsey, 1957, chapter II). Thus he contends that spotting the words 'infinitely' and 'heavenly' (which he calls *qualifiers*) before the words 'good' and 'Father' (*models*, see below Chapter 4) causes us to meditate on a range of people of increasing goodness, or of fathers of various kinds. This continues until a disclosure occurs in which we grasp the concepts of infinite goodness or eternal Fatherhood through a religious experience in which we encounter the divine object to which this language refers. This account of the mechanics of the process seems less convincing for religious language, however, than it does in the illustrations Ramsey provides from mathematics. For example, he describes a situation in which a person who has known only polygons can come to realise what a circle is by being told that a circle is a 'polygon with an infinite number of sides'. 'Infinite polygon' is a phrase that might well generate in the imagination a series of figures with increasing numbers of sides – triangle, square, pentagon, hexagon, etc. – until the 'penny drops' and the 'light dawns' and we have an intuition of a figure *of a different kind altogether* (one with *no* sides), but which is somehow 'generated' by this sequence (cf. Ramsey, 1957, p. 69).

But does something similar happen if you pray, 'Heavenly Father . . .'?

Silence

Beyond the region occupied by the more 'wordy' types of prayer surveyed earlier in this chapter, lies the desert of contemplative prayer. The prayer of adoration approaches this boundary, but doesn't quite reach it. Contemplative prayer is at the limit of all linguistic activity, where every attempt to picture or communicate with God is seen to have broken down, in what is called *apophasis* (see p. 57 below on the *via negativa*). Here human language and all human activity are suspended in a silent waiting upon God, and spiritual writers claim that it is into this silence that the mystery of the God who is beyond words may break. It may seem odd to feature silence in a book about religious language, but in worship, as in prayer more generally, silence is said to be an element as significant as words in evoking and 'realising' the presence of God. (And it is words that frame and lead into the silence.)

But many who pray think of silence as a much more negative thing. The pray-er speaks, but God does not reply.

> I pray and incur
> silence. Some take that silence
> for refusal.
> ('The Presence', Thomas, 1993, p. 391)

In this poem at least, the Welsh poet and priest R S Thomas speaks of silence as the place where the elusive, mysterious power may catch him 'by the sleeve' and guide him to a brief illumination. Some have argued that if this happens, it is because our God-talk has been purified and our words become more authentic. 'In an encounter with divine reality we do not hear a voice but acquire a voice; and the voice we acquire is our own' (Carse, 1985, p. 8). Those who pray speak into the silence, then, and in responding to the silence they come to speak better.

Does God ever speak?

Most accounts of God's role in worship and prayer lead us to expect no more than a passive presence or silent hearer. It is for this reason that many understand the prayer of request primarily in terms of its psychological and spiritual effects on the pray-er. Such prayers serve to strengthen her concern or commitment, and her acceptance of God's will (Phillips, 1965, chapter 6; Ward, 1967, chapter 10). If God is thought of as answering prayers in a less restricted way, it will be *either* by means of God's effect on the intentions, dispositions and behaviour of others (the doctor's skill or the politician's integrity), *or* in terms of a providential steering of – or even a miraculous intervention into – the course of Nature. In all these cases, however, 'God does not in any ordinary sense use language when answering people's prayers' (Moore, 1988, p. 201).

Sometimes, however, people insist that they have received a more direct answer than this, as when Christians in the New Testament, and some charismatic Christians today, report 'words of prophecy', 'words of wisdom' or 'interpretations of tongues' (that is, of glossolalia) that they believe to have come directly from God. Accounts of such phenomena describe thoughts or even words entering the minds of the worshippers with a force, insistence and authority that suggests to the recipient that they come directly from God. This takes us back to the notion of a propositional revelation that we explored in the last chapter. The challenge that all such accounts must face, however, is whether these words – which *at some stage* are human words, thought and spoken by human beings – can be shown to be of divine origin.

The more general question of whether God can truly be said to *speak* is explored in detail by Nicholas Wolterstorff in a different way. Rejecting the usual view that talk of God's speaking is just a metaphorical way of attributing revelation to God, Wolterstorff draws on human parallels. He reminds us that it is quite common for secretaries, ambassadors, deputies and others to write or say something to someone 'in the name of' a third person, where that person supervises or *superintends* the process, or *authorises* or appropriates the text in some other manner. Wolterstorff thinks that the Bible as a whole may be thought of along these lines, 'in terms of divinely appropriated human discourse'. Note that on this account Scripture is recognised as *human* discourse which was in the past a medium of divine discourse, and which may also serve as 'a medium of *contemporary* divine discourse, a medium of God's *here and now* addressing you and me' (Wolterstorff, 1995, p. 53).

So Wolterstorff is thinking here of God 'speaking' by means of the speaking and writing of others. This is not different in principle, he is suggesting, from the executive signing a letter that has been composed and written by her secretary, or the committee member seconding a motion that was composed and spoken by someone else – or, indeed, students and scholars quoting the words of others in their essays and books in order to present their own positions. 'In all such cases, one is appropriating the *text* of the first person as the medium of one's own discourse' (Wolterstorff, 1995, p. 52).

That, perhaps, is one way in which 'God speaks to us' – without, as it were, ever moving his lips, or even having any lips to move (or hands to write texts). It also avoids the worst excesses of the 'divine dictation theory', for on Wolterstorff's model the writing or speaking of the secretary, deputy or ambassador is literally the creation of this person, although it *functions* as the word of the person who superintends or (perhaps later) authorises it. This position surely allows the possibility of error within the human texts of Scripture.

> **EXERCISE**
> What do you think of Wolterstorff's defence of the claim that
> 'God speaks'?

You might look again at the section on revelation at the end of Chapter 2. Wolterstorff calls the non-propositional view of revelation (whether through history or by non-intentional human revelation) 'showing' or 'manifesting', distinguishing it from propositional revelation which is knowledge-transmitting. He distinguishes the latter, however, from God's *speaking*. Wolterstorff argues that much of God's speaking should not count as revelation, for revelation is making known the unknown and dispelling human ignorance about God's nature and acts, whereas in speech God often does a new thing whose purpose is not to inform us of what we do not know, but to issue a command or make a promise (Wolterstorff, 1995, chapter 2).

Further reading

Archbishops' Council (2000), *Common Worship: services and prayers for the Church of England*, London, Church House Publishing.

Gardner, H (1971), Religious poetry, in H Gardner, *Religion and Literature*, pp. 121–142, Oxford, Oxford University Press.

Jasper, D and Jasper, R C D (eds) (1990), *Language and the Worship of the Church*, Basingstoke, Macmillan.

Nichols, B (2000), *Literature in Christian Perspective: becoming faithful readers*, London, Darton, Longman and Todd, especially chapter 3.

Phillips, D Z (1965), *The Concept of Prayer*, London, Routledge and Kegan Paul.

Ramsey, I T (1957), *Religious Language: an empirical placing of theological phrases*, London, SCM, chapter II.

Ramsey, I T (1971), *Our Understanding of Prayer*, London, SPCK.

Smart, N (1972), *The Concept of Worship*, London, Macmillan, part one.

Ward, J N (1967), *The Use of Praying*, London, Epworth.

Watts, F (2001), Prayer and psychology, in F Watts (ed.), *Perspectives on Prayer*, London, SPCK, chapter 4.

Williams, R (2000), *On Christian Theology*, Oxford, Blackwell, chapter 1.

4. METAPHOR, MODEL AND MYTH

Introduction

In her stimulating books *Speaking in Parables* and *Metaphorical Theology*, Sallie McFague (previously TeSelle) makes some big claims about the importance of metaphor in our everyday lives.

> Metaphor is not first of all the language of poets but ordinary language. . . . Language, all language, is ultimately traceable to metaphor – it is the foundation of language and thus of thought. (TeSelle, 1975, pp. 43, 50)

> From the time we are infants we construct our world through metaphor; . . . we constantly ask when we do not know how to think about something, 'What is it like?' Far from being an esoteric or ornamental rhetorical device superimposed *on* ordinary language, metaphor is ordinary language. It is the *way* we think . . . we always think by indirection. (McFague, 1983, pp. 15–16)

In this chapter I want to try to bring together a range of highly significant forms that religious language can take. But let us begin by reflecting on two of the most fundamental within our ordinary language.

Reflecting on experience
How often do you use the 'figurative' language of metaphors and similes in your everyday language? Think back to a recent discussion in which you were involved and try to identify any significant metaphors or similes that were used (by yourself or others).

Figuring it out

Figurative language is any language that uses 'figures of speech' (technically 'tropes'); it is language that is not used literally. Its primary form is *metaphor*. Metaphor has been defined as 'a figure of speech in which one thing, idea, or action is referred to by the name of another' (*Oxford World Encyclopaedia*), or (better) 'whereby we speak about one thing in terms which are seen to be suggestive of another' (Soskice, 1985, p. 15). This reference or application is not literal but imaginative, and suggests some resemblance, similarity or 'common quality' between the two. The word itself derives from the Greek *metapherō*, a combination of *meta* (with, after) and *pherō* (I carry): a metaphor is a carrying over or transfer of a term between one application and another.

There is a long tradition of suspicion of metaphorical language, with many philosophers encouraging the notion that metaphor can be replaced by literal language without loss. Those who have followed this line of reasoning often view metaphor as a 'mere ornament' or substitute, or even as deceptive. (John Locke described the 'figurative application of words' as 'perfect cheats' that 'insinuate wrong ideas'.) Over recent decades, however, the situation has changed, so that many philosophers now treat metaphor as an irreducible and irreplaceable form of language that can give a real, truthful insight into reality.

EXERCISE

Scan whatever instances of writing you have to hand, whether newspapers, novels or works of non-fiction, and try to pick out a few examples of good, illuminating metaphors.

How do you think these metaphors 'work'?

When we employ a metaphor we are in effect bringing together not only two words but two 'worlds', by drawing on two sets of associations or frameworks of meaning. When I use a metaphor I signal to you that I am thinking of *this* subject-matter in terms of *that* linguistic 'figure', 'modifier' or 'vehicle' with its connotations, and this shifts the meaning that is conveyed to 'a resultant of their interaction' (Richards, 1936, p. 93). As the two domains of meaning interact, we might say that one of them 'filters', 'organises' or 'transforms' the other, highlighting some features of the subject and suppressing others, so that something new (a new meaning) is created (cf. Black, 1962, p. 41). Alternatively, we could think of the metaphor as both casting up and organising a network of associations, giving 'new possibilities of vision' (Soskice, 1985, pp. 57–58). To adopt yet another visual image, metaphors may be said to help us to see a new depth through a form of stereoscopic vision in which the two worlds are seen together and transformed, so that we are jolted into seeing similarities that we had not previously noticed.

We should note that in employing such metaphors as 'Man is a wolf' and 'The Lord is my shepherd', *both* elements may be changed or 'reframed'. These metaphors do not simply help us to see human beings and God differently. It is also the case that 'wolves may seem more human-like from now on and it may be that shepherds are viewed with greater consideration after being related to God' (Stiver, 1996, p. 116). The same may be said of the application of the word 'victory' to Jesus' death on the cross (Gunton, 1988, pp. 78–79).

Enthusiasts for metaphor and 'metaphorical theology' assert that a successful metaphor is both *natural* and *fecund*. 'It is an indication of a good metaphor if it is unnecessary to spell out its implications for the reader' (Soskice, 1985, p. 23). This should be a warning to those preachers who are tempted to interrupt their flow in order to explain why they are using a particular figure of speech, rather than just 'letting the metaphor do its job' (TeSelle, 1975, p. 15). (They may be the same people who go on to interrupt repeatedly the congregation's worship in order to explain *why* they are lighting candles or moving to another part of the church, instead of letting these 'natural symbols' speak for themselves.) The good metaphor is also something that we can return to again and again, finding new insights to explore each time (as with the running water metaphor in Scripture and hymnody – see Soskice, 1985, pp. 156–158). For example, describing the camel as 'the ship of the desert' evokes 'limitless suggestions' by considering it on the model of a ship:

> the implied corollaries of a swaying motion, a heavy and precious cargo, a broad wilderness, a route mapped by stars, distant ports of call, and so on. (Soskice, 1985, p. 31)

For reasons such as these, it is argued that it is a profound mistake to seek to reduce metaphors to, and then to replace them by, any 'equivalent' piece of flat, literal, language (the *literalistic fallacy*). Good metaphors cannot be paraphrased or translated without losing much of their point; Janet Martin Soskice insists that 'what is said by the metaphor can be expressed adequately in no other way.'

EXERCISE
Go back to your list of metaphors from the previous exercises and try to translate them into non-metaphorical language. Is anything lost in the translation?

It might be argued that if you did succeed in replacing any of these metaphors by literal expressions then they were not really good metaphors. Perhaps they were examples of language that no longer operates as imaginative metaphors, but has already descended to the level of 'dead metaphors' – as we do when we speak of the 'bonnet' of a car, the 'arm' of a chair, the 'stem' of a glass or the 'leaf' of a book.

A 'live metaphor', on the other hand, has a different metaphorical use when compared with its literal use. It draws attention both to elements of similarity and to elements of difference between two ideas, and thus generates the tension that produces new *cognitive insight*. In addition, it has *affective power*, for it changes the way we feel about that which it labels, and about the label itself. A dead metaphor does neither of these things, hence the claim that it is 'not a metaphor at all, but merely an expression that no longer has a pregnant metaphorical use' (Black, 1979, p. 26). No associations of the concept 'arm' come to mind to clash with what we know about chairs; we don't think of plants when turning the pages of a book.

A metaphorical God?

Scripture is replete with metaphorical language. Such language is used to describe the Church (as body, bride, temple, new Jerusalem), and both faith and faithlessness (as experiencing height, freedom, shade, rest or gift; and being rebels, whores, dead bones or wilting grass). Most significantly, perhaps, it is used to picture the holy, transcendent God.

EXERCISE

Locate as many examples as you can of metaphorical language applied to God in Scripture (a Bible concordance will help).

Try to list them under impersonal and personal metaphors, subdividing each category into different groups.

In many of the examples printed below (mostly stolen from Ramsey, 1971a, pp. 203–205 and Caird, 1980, pp. 154, 174–176) the concept is used but the actual noun does not appear, or the application is to God's spirit, voice or activity rather than directly to God. For example, although God is never directly called a mother, God is portrayed as exercising a mother's care and love.

Impersonal metaphors

INANIMATE NATURE:
rock (Deuteronomy 32:15); fortress, shield, horn, stronghold (Psalm 18:2); fire (Deuteronomy 4:24); light (Psalm 27:1; Isaiah 60:19); sun (Psalm 84:11); thunder (Revelation 14:2); spring (Jeremiah 2:13); wind (Genesis 1:2; John 3:8); soap (Malachi 3:2).

ANIMALS:
lion (Hosea 5:14); leopard, bear (Hosea 13:7–8); bird (Psalm 17:8; Deuteronomy 32:11).

Personal metaphors

HUMAN CRAFTS, ETC. DEALING WITH THINGS AND ANIMALS:
potter (Jeremiah 18:6; Isaiah 64:8); builder (Amos 7:7); silver worker (Malachi 3:3); laundress (Isaiah 4:4); fisherman (Habbakuk 1:15; Matthew 13:47); farmer (Luke 13:6; John 15:1–2; Romans 11:21); shepherd (Ezekiel 34:31); dairymaid (Job 10:10).

CARING PROFESSIONS AND OTHER INTERPERSONAL DEALINGS:
employer (Matthew 20:1); teacher (Jeremiah 31:33–34); physician (Jeremiah 30:17).

NATIONAL LEADERSHIP:
  king (Jeremiah 10:7); warrior (Isaiah 63:5–6);
  judge (Isaiah 33:22; Genesis 18:25).

FAMILY, ETC.:
  father (Jeremiah 3:19; Deuteronomy 32:6; Hosea 11:3–4; Matthew
  5:45, 7:11; John 15:9);
  mother (Deuteronomy 32:18; Isaiah 66:13);
  husband (Hosea 2:16); friend (Jeremiah 3:4).

Model-making

Many philosophers have argued that metaphor has an honourable place
in a number of areas of thought, even including that most carefully
descriptive discipline – natural science. Scientific explanation frequently
employs linguistic *models* to aid understanding. In models 'we regard
one thing or state of affairs in terms of another' (Soskice, 1985, pp.
50–51). A quick glance at such models reveals that they have been developed from illuminating metaphors, and often give rise to other
metaphors. Thus light is said to behave, on some occasions, like 'waves'
propagated across the surface of water, but at others like 'particles' –
miniature billiard balls that travel in straight lines and interact with one
another in a very different fashion. This *imaginative* dimension of
science, in which some significant similarity is recognised between two
apparently unrelated things, is a central feature of scientific discovery
(Hesse, 1954). Scientific models form a major element in what Thomas
Kuhn has called scientific *paradigms* and Imre Lakatos has labelled
research programmes: essentially, basic ways of doing science, such as
Newtonian physics or Darwinian biology (see Barbour, 1974; Banner,
1990).

All models may be thought of as systematically developed, stable and
long-lasting metaphors (Max Black, Sallie McFague) or analogies (Ian
Barbour), which have the potential to organise and structure our thinking, and to suggest possibilities for its development. (We will consider
the distinction between metaphors and analogies in the next chapter.)
McFague treats models as occupying a sort of intermediate point or
'further step along the route from metaphorical to conceptual language'
(McFague, 1983, p. 23). They thus retain many characteristics of the
metaphor, including interpretative potential, while serving as a filter for

organising our thinking and reasoning about something unfamiliar by helping us to see it in more familiar terms.

Models are commonplace in religious discourse. Think, for example, of the model of 'person', which theology applies to God both when it says that God is 'personal' and when it distinguishes the three 'persons' of the Trinity. Think also of the various models proposed for creation: for example, emanation and procreation; or architect, painter, speaker and novelist (Astley, 2000a, chapter 2).

The ever-present danger as we move away from the more obviously figurative metaphors to modes of thought that are more conceptual is that we forget that *A* is not *really B*: that there is dissimilarity as well as similarity between the idea or model and the reality it seeks to represent. 'The price of the employment of models', it has been said, 'is eternal vigilance' (Braithwaite, 1968, p. 93). It is usually obvious that metaphors are not to be taken literally, and we are on the whole content to place them alongside other metaphors. But we are more tempted to take models literally and, having endorsed one, to refuse to acknowledge the relevance of other models. For example, whereas Scripture and liturgy throw together a variety of metaphors of the death of Christ (victory, sacrifice, ransom), the theology of atonement argues over whether the death of Christ is best seen on the model of a conquest over evil powers, an example to others, a satisfaction for the dishonour of sin *or* a penal substitution. As the example of the wave and particle models illustrates, however, science at least is willing to allow *complementary models*, recognising that each on its own is incomplete, but that the two cannot be synthesised into some coherent super-model. It may be that Nature is so mysterious and paradoxical that we need to keep on using two very different ways of speaking about it, despite the tensions between the two. So why not do the same with God?

Models give rise to abstract *concepts* which, although they possess metaphorical roots, rarely reveal them. The richness of metaphors is related to their indirect, allusive nature and their diversity; concepts are constructed so as to have meanings that are as direct, clear, concise and unambiguous as possible. In theology, as in other areas of thought, both figurative variety and literal clarity may be needed.

> The relationship . . . is symbiotic. Images 'feed' concepts; concepts 'discipline' images. Images without concepts are blind; concepts without images are sterile. In a metaphorical theology, there is no suggestion of a hierarchy among metaphors, models, and concepts: concepts are not

higher, better, or more necessary than images, or vice versa. Images are never free of the need for interpretation by concepts, their critique of competing images, or their demythologizing of literalized models. Concepts are never free of the need for funding by images, the affectional and existential richness of images, and the qualification against conceptual pretensions supplied by the plurality of images. (McFague, 1983, p. 26)

Therefore, 'doctrine, necessary and appropriate as it is, does not replace the metaphors that fund it' (p. 50).

The point of models

But what, we may ask, is the point or status of models, either in science or in theology? A number of very different answers to that question have been proposed.

The traditional answer is a form of *realism*, which is understood in this context as the view that our language can properly represent reality. Naïve realism assumes that it does this by a straightforward picturing relationship between reality ('the facts') and our models. *Critical realists*, however, acknowledge that human language can never offer a literal description of the elusive entities of science or theology, while insisting that it does allow an approximate representation of them. Although both the atom and God are 'nonpicturable but real' (McFague, 1983, p. 97), we may speak of 'reality depiction' in science and theology as they both refer to a reality outside themselves (Soskice, 1985, chapters VI–VIII). Thus 'valid theories are true as well as useful', and models are 'neither pictures of reality nor useful fictions; they are partial and inadequate ways of imagining what is not observable' (Barbour, 1974, pp. 37, 48). On this account of the matter, our scientific and religious language is never wholly adequate, but it does offer us partial and revisable – but nonetheless genuine – accounts of the world and of God. We therefore need to be cautious, tentative, indefinite, even agnostic, in using such language, for it is never directly descriptive, even though it does refer to and represent reality. We need 'a duly humble and listening language' that reflects 'a combination of openness and mystery, speech and silence' (Gunton, 1988, pp. 37–38).

Instrumentalism, the radical alternative view, treats models as no more than 'heuristic fictions'. This means that they assist discovery by acting as techniques for predicting observations or aids to theorising, but can (and should) be replaced by neat and tidy concepts and theories – or even mathematical equations. Such models are ultimately expendable: useful for making discoveries, but not really helpful in explaining anything. They do not represent real entities in the world at all. Even more radical are the *positivists* (see Chapter 6 below) who argue that theories and models can be reduced and replaced by lists of observations. At the other extreme, *idealists* treat models as human inventions that only exist in our minds, and which we impose on our experience without their representing anything outside themselves.

Model-mixing

EXERCISE
📖 **Read Psalms 89:26; Isaiah 9:2–6; Revelation 21:2.**

List all the different metaphorical models in these texts.

According to Ramsey, heresy results from fastening on one model to understand God and running it to death, whereas 'orthodoxy is aimed at having every possible model' (Ramsey, 1957, p. 170). At the less rigorous level of primary religious language, this involves the 'piling up of models' or 'jostling' of metaphors, as when Jesus is spoken of in the hymn as shepherd, prophet, priest, husband, friend and king (Ramsey, 1963, p. 10).

McFague is similarly appreciative of multi-model discourse. To avoid the danger of neglecting to recognise the element of dissimilarity in a model, and therefore of equating model and reality, we must embrace a plurality of models. She writes of the value of a theology that is created from a network of models that qualify one another, for no one model can encompass the richness of the divine-human relationship (McFague, 1983, pp. 139–144).

God in story form

Theology in the English-speaking world has found 'story' a useful concept in a number of ways. It is neutral as between an account of actual events (history) and imaginative fiction, from both of which theologians believe important theological truth can derive. It leads to placing the stress, in biblical studies, on the narrative dimension of texts rather than on their 'doctrinal' content. This can be a liberation from too didactic a reading of Scripture. It brings Christian theology potentially closer to Judaism, where the narration of the saving events (above all, in the Exodus and gift of the Promised Land) has a central place in theological understanding. (Sauter and Barton, 2000, p. 3)

The story form is also central to our self-understanding, and to our understanding of life, the universe and everything; we are, it has been said, inherently 'story-shaped' – 'we emplot ourselves as we go' (Stiver, 2001, p. 167). (See Chapter 10 below.) According to William Bausch, 'story is the stuff of life'; and while 'theology is secondhand reflection of . . . an event', it is story that is 'the unspeakable event's first voice' (Bausch, 1984, p. 28). *Narrative theology* lays particular stress on how the identity of Jesus and God are given within biblical and mythic narratives (e.g. Frei, 1975; Hauerwas and Jones, 1989), for 'it is through the Christian story that God speaks' (Wilder, 1964, p. 64).

Parables
Jesus' preferred mode of teaching, at least in the Synoptic gospels, is through parables. These are secular stories about ordinary people and things that work as extended metaphors with plots, *story-metaphors*. The fact that Jesus often introduces his parables with the phrase, 'The Kingdom of God [or heaven] is *like* . . .' (e.g. Matthew 13:31–50; Mark 4:26–32) suggests that, technically speaking, many parables are *similes*. However, as such similes often function just like (explicit) metaphors, we may agree that 'a parable is an extended metaphor' (TeSelle, 1975, pp. 67, 79). Parables, of course, are usually products of the imagination, and best categorised as 'fictitious' or 'fictive', although a recent empirical study suggests that a surprisingly high proportion of churchgoers think that they narrate historical events (Village, 2003, pp. 93–109).

Parables often involve tensions. Like metaphors they bring together very dissimilar worlds, as when the Kingdom of God is compared with seeds or buried treasure. Alternatively, expectations are overturned in the world of the metaphor, as in the parables of the Great Feast (Luke 13:15–24) and the Unjust Steward (Luke 16:1–8). Those who heard them are likely to have undergone 'a somewhat unnerving experience' of disorientation and unease. Parables 'are meant to change, not reassure us'; they 'shatter the deep structures of our accepted world . . . remove our defences and make us vulnerable to God'. 'I don't know what you mean by that story but I'm certain I don't like it' (Crossan, 1975, pp. 56, 122). One of the most significant features of the parable is the way that it can 'disarm' the listeners: 'We are drawn into the story and, before we discover our defences have been lowered, the message has penetrated' (Evans, 1999, p. 76).

EXERCISE
📖 Read 2 Samuel 11:2 to 12:15; Matthew 20:1–16; Luke 18:9–14.

How do you react to these stories? How might their original audience have reacted to them?

I am reminded of a Sunday lunchtime argument with a house guest who questioned the morality of that vineyard owner paying the same wage to those he hired late as he gave to those who had worked all day in the sun. The shock of the story must have been the same for its first hearers, but those who have heard it repeatedly probably miss the point entirely. (The real point, however, is that if the employer had paid any less, the labourer and his family would all have starved. Thus God's grace and generosity overturn our moralities of just desert and fair rewards.) I also recall a disastrous children's sermon during which I retold the parable of the Pharisee and the tax-collector, complete with expensive puppets. Having gone into some detail about the religious virtues of the former and the secular vices of the latter, I dramatically acted out their different prayers. When prompted, my congregation spoke out with one voice – in condemnation of the tax-collector. I was much chastened, but only because *I* had lost the plot. Of course the tax-collector was the baddy, that was the point of telling the story; he was a baddy who was justified by God because of his humility. The kids were reacting as Jesus must have expected his original listeners to react, before he hit them with the punchline of verse 14. The story had wrong-footed them, as Jesus intended it to. I had been misled by the reaction of adult church-goers who, having heard this parable too often, miss the tension of the tale. It no longer generates any shock because, after all, *we* expect Pharisees to be condemned – arrogant hypocrites that they are! (See Thiselton, 1980, pp. 14–15.)

Myth understood?

The everyday meaning of the word 'myth' is a 'widely-held but false notion' – a meaning that is also to be found in the New Testament (see 1 Timothy 4:7; 2 Peter 1:16). This is liable to cause religious believers to resist the claim that any biblical passage or theological narrative is a myth. But scholars do not use the word in this way. Most often it refers to a significant narrative that speaks of the activity of God or other supernatural figures in human and mundane terms, often picturing God visiting the world and interacting with human beings. Whereas much religious language provides a 'static picture' of God and God's activities, using metaphors and analogies (e.g. 'God is a loving Father'), myths put together these 'stills' to produce a 'movie' in which God's activity is presented in story form (e.g. 'God came down from heaven to be born in a stable' and 'God will roll up the universe at the end of time'). 'Myths constellate sacred symbolism in narrative sequence' (Avis, 1999, p. 125). Religions employ these particular story-metaphors in order to speak about the activity of another divine world and its impact on our world. Ninian Smart has a striking definition of myth as 'a moving picture of the sacred' (Smart, 1973, p. 79). Not only does this capture the 'motion' of a story, it also suggests the powerful influence such stories have on the adherents of the religion in which they are found. Myths have enormous emotional power; people live by, and sometimes die for, their myths (cf. Smart, 1996, chapter 3).

But should we *believe* them? It is usually said that a myth, like a metaphor, is not literally true. God (or Christ) did not literally come down at Christmas, any more than God is literally a father (Swinburne, 1992, pp. 159–161). If we were to view the myth at a literal, surface level, we would be tempted to say that it is untrue. Nevertheless, it contains a deeper truth about God's activities, by using the narrative in a non-literal way.

EXERCISE
📖 Read Genesis 2:4–25 and 11:1–9; John 1:1–18;
    Philippians 2:5–11.

What truths (religious, moral, spiritual, theological, metaphysical, historical) are expressed in these mythic narratives?

In what sense then do they represent claims about what, 'as a
matter of fact', happened or is the case?

These are difficult questions to answer. Liberal theologians have suggested various ways of assessing the truth of a myth.
• John Hick defines a religious myth as:

> a story which is not literally true, or an identifying concept or image
> which does not literally apply, but which may be 'true' in virtue of its
> power to evoke an appropriate attitude. (Hick, 1973, p. 175)

In a way this account does not get us much further, because we still
need to ask, 'What is an appropriate attitude?' and 'Why is this attitude
appropriate?' The myths that God came down to earth in Christ and
defeated the powers of evil may evoke confidence and gratitude, but
many would argue that these attitudes cannot be said to be appropriate unless something has *happened* in response to which I ought to feel
grateful and confident.
• Maurice Wiles holds that 'there must be some ontological truth corre-
sponding to the central characteristic of the structure of the myth'
(Wiles, 1977, p. 161). Thus the Genesis myth of the creation of the
universe in six days incorporates the deep ontological truth (that is,
truth about being or reality) that the universe is dependent now on
God for its existence. Similarly, the myth of the Fall – that Adam and
Eve fell from grace in the Garden of Eden – incorporates the truth that
all human beings are oriented away from the will of God. But can a
myth be translated without remainder into such a contemporary, universal 'theological truth'? Some would argue that, quite apart from any
possible historical anchoring of the myth, some stories cannot be
rewritten in a non-story form without loss (Sykes, 1979; cf. Astley,
1981).
• Rudolph Bultmann notably argued that we should *demythologise* the

New Testament, by translating its mythology into the language of existential (personal) decision. He insisted that the objective form of biblical myths is misleading for the modern reader who simply cannot believe in a three-storey universe of heaven, earth and hell, in which supernatural powers intervene in human history. Demythologising involves re-interpreting myths by 'asking for the deeper meaning of mythological conceptions and freeing the Word of God from a by-gone world-view' (Bultmann, 1960, p. 43).

> To believe in the cross of Christ does not mean to concern ourselves with a mythical process wrought outside of us and our world, with an objective event turned by God to our advantage, but rather to make the cross of Christ our own, to undergo crucifixion with him. (Bultmann, 1964, p. 36)

Myths have their effect in a very personal way. Religious myths are not like scientific facts or theories, which do not involve our hearts and wills. They do not function 'objectively'; for a myth to 'work', it must work for you. The language of myth is therefore *self-involving* language. The affirmation of a mythic statement 'can only be a personal confession . . . It cannot be made as a neutral statement, but only as thanksgiving and surrender' (Bultmann, 1960, p. 69). Whether recognising this personal dimension necessitates such a radical treatment of myth is, however, widely questioned.

What do you think?

Further reading

Avis, P (1999), *God and the Creative Imagination: metaphor, symbol and myth in religion and theology*, London, Routledge.

Barbour, I G (1974), *Myths, Models and Paradigms: the nature of scientific and religious language*, London, SCM.

Caird, G B (1980), *The Language and Imagery of the Bible*, London, Duckworth, chapters 8 and 13.

Crossan, J D (1975), *The Dark Interval: towards a theology of story*, Allen, Texas, Argus.

Evans, R (1999), *Using the Bible: studying the text*, London, Darton, Longman and Todd, chapters 5 and 7.

McFague, S (1983), *Metaphorical Theology*, London, SCM.

Perrin, N (1976), *Jesus and the Language of the Kingdom: symbol and metaphor in New Testament interpretation*, London, SCM.

Ramsey, I T (1957), *Religious Language: an empirical placing of theological phrases*, London, SCM.

Ramsey, I T (1964), *Models and Mystery*, Oxford, Oxford University Press.

Ramsey, I T (1973), *Models for Divine Activity*, London, SCM.

Soskice, J M (1985), *Metaphor and Religious Language*, Oxford, Oxford University Press.

Stiver, D R (1996), *The Philosophy of Religious Language: sign, symbol and story*, Oxford, Blackwell, chapter 6.

TeSelle, S M (1975), *Speaking in Parables: a study in metaphor and theology*, London, SCM.

5. ANALOGIES, TRUTH AND MYSTERY

Introduction

In the last chapter we looked at figurative ways of talking about God. Much religious language speaks about God's nature, character and activities in this mode. But many argue that the reach of religious language does not stop there. We need to talk of God in a more straightforward manner; we need to apply some language to God *literally*.

According to the dictionary, the word 'literal' means 'taking words in their usual and most basic sense'; literal speech is 'accustomed speech' (Soskice, 1985, p. 69). This primary sense is to be distinguished from the metaphorical sense we explored above, but also from simile, hyperbole, irony, satire, allegory, and so on. When people stress that they are speaking literally, they don't want us to assume that they are 'only' using some sort of figurative expression. They insist that they 'really' mean what they are saying about God.

Reflecting on experience

Brian Davies writes: 'Someone might say, "God is a mighty fortress". We then ask, "Is that really true? Is God made of stone, for example?" The answer will probably be: "Of course not. I am speaking metaphorically." ... But suppose someone now says "God is alive" or "God is good". Again we ask, "Is that really true? Is he really alive and good? Or are we now using a figure of speech?"' (Davies, 1993, pp. 22–23.)

From your experience, how would people respond to these questions? How do you respond to them?

There is a problem in making 'really (true)' equivalent to 'literally (true)', for some may wish to say that God is 'really' a father or 'truly' a fortress, while acknowledging that these are metaphors. Perhaps a better way of expressing the difference would be that believers are quite happy to say, 'Of course God is not in the usual sense of the word a fortress', but not to say, 'Naturally, I don't mean that God is good in the usual sense.' This is an important distinction between two different ways of describing God, which we shall need to examine more closely. (Confusingly, in recent years a colloquial or informal usage has developed in which people sometimes speak of a metaphorical expression as being 'literally' true, when they only mean to add emphasis to it. For example, 'We received a literal avalanche of mail.')

It is often thought that a literal understanding of religious language was the original practice of those who read, and who wrote, Scripture and that we ought to follow biblical fundamentalists in returning to 'the literal word of God'. Several points need to be made here.

- Fundamentalists, who take their name from a nineteenth-century 'back to basics' reaction against liberal theology in North America, are marked more by the claim that all the Bible is inerrant (that is, cannot be wrong), rather than that it is all to be taken literally. Indeed, they are often forced to adopt metaphorical interpretations of biblical texts such as the 'six days' of creation in order to defend their claims for inerrancy (see Barr, 1981, pp. 40–55).
- The Bible itself is full of obvious and uncontroversial metaphors and similes. Thus Jesus preaches about his 'Father', speaks of himself as a 'vine' and 'door' of the sheepfold, and says that the Kingdom of God is like a mustard seed or a costly pearl. God's hand, voice and outstretched arm were never intended to be taken literally; nor can anyone literally *see* God (John 1:18; cf. Exodus 33:17–23).
- From the third century at least, Christians were encouraged to read the Bible at a number of different levels. A reference to 'Jerusalem' could be taken *literally* or historically (as the earthly city), or in one of three different spiritual senses: *allegorically* (as the Christian Church), *tropologically* or morally (the soul), or *anagogically* or eschatologically (the future heavenly city of God).
- Augustine argued that the author of Genesis had to write in metaphors or allegories because his readers were untutored in science; as John Calvin later put it, God 'adapts his discourse to common usage'.

Metaphor, analogy and literal talk

According to Aquinas, words like 'wise', 'good' and 'living' are used ana-logically. An *analogy* expresses a 'partial similarity' or, to put it more vividly, 'a certain likeness in difference . . . a mean between extremes' (Anderson, 1949, p. 19). When applied to God, such words are used with a similar meaning, but not an identical meaning, to the meaning they have when they are applied to human beings. They are said to be used literally, but analogically, of God. To put it in Aquinas' own words (Aquinas, *Summa Theologiae*, 1a, 13, 3; Vol. 3, 1964, p. 59), analogies are words that 'simply mean certain perfections without any indication of how these perfections are possessed – words, for example, like "being", "good", "living" and so on. These words can be used literally of God.' In this way, metaphor's *figurative* language is radically distinguished from analogy's *literal* (but 'stretched' or 'extended') meaning. Words like 'rock' and 'lion' cannot be applied literally to God since they are thought to have material limitations built in to their meaning: 'it is part of the meaning of "rock" that it has its being in a merely material way. Such words can be used of God only metaphorically.'

> [For St Thomas] when you 'try to mean' God's goodness by using the word 'good' of him, you are not straying outside its normal meaning but trying to enter more deeply into it. His objection to the metaphor theory of theological language is that in metaphor the primary use of the word is a literal one, so that words would always apply primarily to creatures and to use them of God would be to move outside their ordi-nary meaning. (McCabe, 1964, p. 107)

It is for these reasons that Aquinas and others believe that analogy is greatly to be preferred over metaphor. This is the exact opposite of the position of those we met in Chapter 4, who rank metaphors much more highly. They treat linguistic analogy as non-creative, preferring the gen-uine innovation and insight that comes from metaphorical talk and its 'imaginative strain' (Soskice, 1985, p. 66). However, some contemporary writers (e.g. David Tracy) write of analogy and metaphor almost inter-changeably, and give an account of analogy that makes many of the same positive points about irreducibility, fertility and originality that others make of metaphors. Others treat the difference between analogy and metaphor as one of degree rather than of kind, suggesting a continuous spectrum of shifted meaning, and sometimes regarding metaphors as the more dispensable usage (Hesse, 1954, p. 145; Smart, 1979, p. 66).

'Metaphorical thinking is nothing but a special case of analogical think-ing' (Ross, 1998, p. 132). Don Stiver comments that 'it is arguable that metaphor, analogy, and symbol can be seen as very similar, and it is arguable that they are very different' (Stiver, 1996, p. 127).

Specifying our God-talk

EXERCISE

It is often claimed that analogies are more appropriate than metaphors in theological *argument*. Why might this be?

The problem of evil, to take one example, is a problem in theology only because we assume that if we say that God is wise, powerful and loving, certain implications follow about how God will treat his crea-tures (see Astley, 2000a, pp. 60–61). The justification for this is that, in Davies' phrase, God is *really* like this. But can we reason from *metaphors* in this way? Can we spell out as clearly what follows from calling God a father, king, shepherd or dairymaid – or a rock, lion or shield?

Well, *something* must be implied by such metaphors, otherwise they would never have been employed. It may be that analogies work better in arguments than metaphors do because metaphors 'have very vague meanings', whereas at least some words are used analogically with 'fairly clear and precise senses' (Swinburne, 1992, p. 50). But this difference appears to be only a difference in degree, and Richard Swinburne argues elsewhere that, once we give analogical senses to a word it is the harder to deduce conclusions from statements concerning that word, 'for words used in analogical senses have wide applications and woolly boundaries'. His advice, therefore, is that the theologian should not play the analog-ical card too often, but be sure to use many other words of God in perfectly ordinary senses (Swinburne, 1977, pp. 61–62, 70). (For more on this, see pp. 61–63 below.) Humphrey Palmer writes:

> I say that analogy is almost as bad for arguments as is outright ambi-guity. If a term means something *partly* different when applied to God, and if we cannot say how different its meaning then becomes, then any argument in which it plays a part is unreliable *for us*. Then I argue . . . that as terms are applied to God here below only by analogy, argu-

mentative theology cannot exist as a descriptive science. (Palmer, 1973, p. 141, cf. p. 98)

Many would agree that, even in the case of analogies, we can infer nothing at all from religious language without *specifying our terms*. Nothing follows from the claim that 'God is loving' unless we can say in what ways God's love is (and is not) like our love. We know what is implied by saying that another person is loving: he or she will feel certain things, do certain things and not do other things. But what is implied by saying that *God* is loving?

Aquinas recognised that analogical terms have both an *affirmative* and a *negative component*. It is crucial to any proper use of analogy that we acknowledge both elements:

> The positive content of an analogy consists of that which it has in common with that for which it stands. The negative content consists of those features which are not shared. In addition to similarity, there is dissimilarity. The extent to which there is correspondence determines the strength and usefulness of an analogy. (Fawcett, 1970, p. 55)

EXERCISE

What are the positive and negative elements in the words 'life' and 'knowledge' when they are applied analogically to God?

You might say that God is 'living' or 'alive' in that God is an agent who is aware of others. But you will probably want to add that, as infinite Spirit, existing without a body and therefore not 'in' space (or even, perhaps, time), God does *not* possess most of the defining characteristics of biological life – such as reproduction, irritability and movement, or growth and development. Similarly, because God is not subject to the limitations to which we ourselves are subject, God's knowledge is not acquired in the same ways (through learning and experience), and is not restricted in the same ways (fallible and limited), as is our own all-too-human knowledge.

When the ambiguity of an analogy has been clarified in this fashion it may be incorporated into a valid argument, for we now know something of what it implies and what it does not imply (see Hayner, 1958; Alston, 1989, chapter 1). However, even after going through such an exercise, many would insist that we are still employing analogies in saying that God is 'alive' or 'wise'; we are not applying the term to human beings and God with exactly the same meaning. But the analogy is now more specific, and therefore more useful.

We should also notice, however, that the more we specify or explain our theological analogies, the less room we leave for mystery. For this reason, many religious believers refuse to say too much, or to be too specific in their God-talk. But there is an obvious price to pay for thus safeguarding God's mystery.

Locating analogy

Analogy is often presented as a middle way of applying human language to God, 'a mean between extremes'. But what are these extremes?

A word might be applied to both human beings and God in one of two very different ways:

- *univocally*: that is, with exactly the same meaning (from the Latin *vocare*, 'call' plus *unus*, 'one' – thus 'with a single voice'); or
- *equivocally*: that is, with completely different meanings (from *vocare* plus *equi-*, 'equal' – thus 'double voiced'). (To 'equivocate' is to use ambiguity to conceal the truth, a technique in which politicians are often skilled.)

EXERCISE
With the help of a dictionary, try to find some clear examples of words that are used equivocally: that is, words that have two or more wholly different – and *unrelated* – literal meanings. These 'ambiguous' words, 'of double or doubtful meaning', will be applied to wholly different sorts of things.

There are lots of them, including 'bank', 'bat', 'light', 'rape', 'tap' and 'rose'. In fact the majority of English words are applied to more than one type of object or situation, and therefore can be used to convey different meanings. (Only technical terms such as 'electron', 'semiconductor' and 'DNA' seem to escape this fate.) One reason for this is that there are more things (and relationships, qualities, activities, etc.) in the world than there are words in our language to apply to them. Where these meanings are completely different and unrelated, they illustrate 'equivocity'. Of course, you will also have come across lots of examples where one word has a 'normal' meaning and application but is also applied as a *metaphor* or *analogy* to describe something that is similar to it in some way; unlike equivocal language, these uses are clearly related to, and appear as modifications of, the normal use.

God-talk on the tightrope

EXERCISE

It is often said that applying human language to God *either* univocally (with exactly the same meaning) *or* equivocally (with completely different meanings) leads to problems. What might these problems be?

Many claim that if language about human beings is applied univocally to God, theology becomes *anthropomorphic*: that is, God is thought of as 'having a human form' (Greek, *anthrōpos*, 'human being'; *morph*, 'form'). God is then pictured as being exactly like a human being, and 'Our Heavenly Father' becomes 'Big Daddy in the Sky'. But, as Ludwig Wittgenstein rhetorically asked, 'Are eyebrows going to be talked of, in connection with the Eye of God?' (Wittgenstein, 1966, p. 71).

If language about human beings is used wholly equivocally of God, however, describing God becomes impossible. If words such as father, wise and good have a completely different meaning when applied to God, we will be left with the silence of *agnosticism*; for we will not know what we mean by religious language, only what we don't mean by it. (For whatever it now means, this bears no resemblance to what the same words meant when applied to humans.)

Several steps beyond such equivocation lies a traditional method of doing theology that is described as the *via negativa* ('the negative way'). It advises that we strip away all human or finite images from our talk about God. In such a perspective, God is thought of as ineffable or indescribable; strictly speaking all that we can say is that God is 'not this' and 'not that'. Pursued vigorously, this approach would lead us to say that God is an utter and total mystery of which we can give no positive account whatever.

But let us return to the positive ways in which language may be applied to God. Aquinas rejects both (pure) equivocation and (simple) univocal predication for God-talk. Although he allowed that certain abstract negative descriptions, such as 'eternal' (outside time) or 'immaterial (without a material body) might be predicated of God without change of meaning, he argued that otherwise 'it is impossible to predicate anything univocally of God and creatures.' His preferred doctrine of *analogical predication* involves applying concrete positive terms to God with a similar meaning to that which these words and phrases normally have when they are applied to us. Their meaning when applied to God is not exactly the same as, but nor is it totally different from, their 'normal' meaning. This limited shift in meaning allows us to avoid both the anthropomorphism of univocal predication and the agnosticism of the equivocal use of language. (In fact, Aquinas thought of analogy as a sort of qualified equivocal language, rejecting only 'pure' or 'sheer' equivocity in speaking about God.)

Employing theological language analogically is like walking a tightrope. You can fall over on one side if your God-talk becomes too anthropomorphic – into the pit of univocity and anthropomorphism. Or you can fall off on the other side, falling into equivocity and agnosticism, by allowing your language to change its ordinary meaning so much when you apply it to God that it ceases to mean anything specific at all. The trick is to tread the tightrope between these two abysses. Most God-talkers tend to lean over to one side or the other, and some frequently overbalance.

The chicken-egg dilemma in analogy

In discussing a word such as 'wise', we might ask which comes first: its application to God or its use of humans? The traditional answer is that in the 'order of knowing' (Latin, *ordo cognoscendi*) we learn the ordinary meaning of words first and then apply them 'upwards' to God. But in the 'order of being' (*ordo essendi*) God always comes first, creating the world (and human beings in particular) in his likeness, and thus giving rise to an 'analogy of being' (*analogia entis*) between creator and creation. As God is the cause of the human qualities that we call 'goodness' and 'wisdom', it is said that these words apply primarily and more properly to God, and only secondarily to us. But this is only in terms of the 'reality signified'. In terms of their 'way of signifying', 'wise' and 'good' properly apply to humans and only secondly and improperly to God.

Karl Barth rejected St Thomas' analogy of being in favour of an 'analogy of faith' (*analogia fidei*), arguing that the resemblance of human theology to the reality of God is accomplished only in faith and by God's grace. The *analogia entis* – the 'divine likeness of the creature even in the fallen world' (Barth, 1975, p. 41) – must be rejected, since God can only be known by his gracious revelation of himself and not through our study of the world. Hence the order of knowing is reversed for Barth: the *proper* meaning of 'father' is as a description of *God*; it is God who selects this word and reveals it to us as the correct way to do theology. On this account, the human understanding of 'father' is no help to us in getting us started in talking about God.

Barth's approach has been welcomed for forcing us to rethink our conception of God through his 'simple but resolute refusal to look else-where than to God's self-revelation to learn what He is like' (White, 1982, p. 224). Many others, however, argue that this position can result in a pure equivocity between the meaning of 'father' when applied to humans and when applied to God. If these words have completely different meanings, then the homely ordinary meaning that we learned as a child is of no use to us in our God-talk.

What do you think?

Types of analogy

Thomists (followers of St Thomas Aquinas) distinguish between two types of analogy.

The analogy of (proper) proportionality
This form of analogy, which seems to have been the more important one for Aquinas, depends on the idea of a 'proportionality'. This is a relationship between two relationships, such as '1 is to 3 as 2 is to 6' (which can be expressed as 1:3::2:6), or 'hand is to glove as foot is to sock' (hand:glove::foot:sock). How on earth is this going to help?

We frequently use analogical language to speak of our pets. In calling Fido 'happy' and 'faithful', we imply that 'happiness' and 'faithfulness' in a dog are similar to these properties in ourselves, the difference being explained by the different natures of dogs and humans. In theology we appeal to the same sort of relationship. For example, God is 'alive' or 'wise' *in God's way*, as we are alive and wise in our way. We might say, then, that as the life of human beings is determined by the nature of human beings in a way that is proper to human beings, so the life of God is determined by the nature of God in a way that is proper to God. There is no *direct* analogy between human life and divine 'life', but there is a 'relational likeness': divine life is related to the divine nature as human life is related to human nature. (Again, A is to B as C is to D.)

Now this sort of thing works very well with dogs, because we have some idea of the possibilities and limitations of a dog's nature. But in the case of God, not only do we not know what divine life is like, we are ignorant of the divine nature as well. And in the proportionality A:B::C:D, if C and D are known but *both* A and B are unknown, the analogy cannot really help us to 'find A' (in this case, what 'life' means when applied to God). For this reason, Thomists often supplement the analogy of proportionality by the use of our next type of analogy (Mascall, 1966, chapter 5).

The analogy of attribution

We often use analogy in speaking of such things as 'healthy' climates and diets. These are not in themselves healthy, but we describe them in this way because they cause good health in people. This is the analogy of attribution (or, sometimes, 'proportion'). This form of analogy will not get us very far in our God-talk on its own, unfortunately, if all it claims is that God is ('virtually') 'wise' in that he is the cause of wisdom in human beings (who are 'actually' wise). Certainly our everyday observations of causes and effects suggest to us that healthy foods and resorts are not themselves rosy-cheeked or energetic. But Aquinas also argued that effects necessarily *resemble* their causes, and that everything created is therefore 'a created analogue of its author' (Anderson, 1949, p. 310). This understanding of analogy thus depends on the idea of an analogy of being between the creator and his creation. St Thomas writes:

> Any creature, in so far as it possesses any perfection, represents God and is like to him, for he, being simply and universally perfect, has pre-existing in himself the perfections of all his creatures. (Aquinas, *Summa Theologiae*, 1a, 13, 2; Vol. 3, 1964, p. 55)

We can perhaps see what Aquinas is driving at; but the idea that effects obviously pre-exist potentially in their causes, and somehow therefore in a more perfect manner, is one that most of us would not share. Lacking Aquinas' metaphysical assumptions, we are likely to respond that clever, good-looking children don't always have parents who have similar qualities. In any case, since God creates *all* creatures and all their attributes, this principle is in danger of licensing us to say far too much about God. Perhaps that problem can be solved, however, by concentrating on the human creation, which is explicitly said to be made in God's image (Genesis 1:27).

Speaking of God in one voice

When we were exploring the different ways in which language might be applied to God, you might have questioned the claim that we cannot apply any such language univocally.

What about the phrase, 'creator of heaven and earth out of nothing'? This might be regarded as a technical description that applies only to God, and not to human beings or other created things. 'Omnipotent' (all-powerful) might be another. In such cases, admittedly, we cannot say that the terms apply 'with one voice' to *both* humans and God, but at least we can say that they have only one proper meaning.

But even this may not be true, as such language *is* sometimes also used of humans. For example, the Roman Emperor was called 'omnipotent', and a writer or fashion designer may be said to be 'creative'. We may think of *these* examples as extended (analogical) uses of technical theological language that normally or properly only apply to God. Or we can understand them in a different way, by saying that such language employs terms that only properly apply to human beings and is therefore being used analogically when it is applied to God. It might then be said that human beings are the ones who create things in the normal sense (that is, design and make them out of something else), and that God analogically 'creates' (that is, designs and makes things out of nothing). Similarly, human beings may be said to be powerful ('potent') in the standard sense, whereas God is only analogically powerful. On the whole, however, you may prefer to treat fully-qualified, technical theological phrases, such as 'creator of all things out of nothing', 'infinitely powerful', and so on, as terms that only have 'one proper meaning', and only one proper application – God.

In the above analysis I have tried hard to avoid contrasting an analogical use of a word or phrase with a 'literal' use, in recognition of the claim that analogy is itself a literal use of language (see above p. 53). But you might notice in other books that what I have labelled as 'normal', 'standard' or 'fully literal' (as distinct from an analogical application), others may refer to just as 'literal'. But if analogy is a form of literal talk, this is imprecise. (It is also worth remarking that in the dictionaries the literal sense or application, understood as the 'usual', 'primary' or 'most basic' one, is normally distinguished from any figurative use. But it may also be contrasted with 'exaggeration' and 'distortion', and I suppose that *might* be allowed to cover analogy.)

For a defence of the view that some words may be predicated of God in a truly univocal way, we may turn to an argument from William Alston. He provides a useful list of 'various ways in which creaturely terms can be used in speaking of God', noting that a number of them have routinely been ruled out by different commentators on religious language because of God's transcendence or 'otherness'. These ways include:

(1) *Straight univocity.* Ordinary terms are used in the same ordinary senses of God and human beings.

(2) *Modified univocity.* Meanings can be defined or otherwise established such that terms can be used with those meanings of both God and human beings.

(3) *Special literal meanings.* Terms can be given, or otherwise take on, special technical senses in which they apply only to God.

(4) *Analogy.* Terms for creatures can be given analogical extensions so as to be applicable to God.

(5) *Metaphor.* Terms that apply literally to creatures can be metaphorically applied to God.

(6) *Symbol.* Ditto for 'symbol', in one or another meaning of that term.

(Alston, 1987, p. 22)

Alston comments that 'the most radical partisans of otherness, from Dionysius through Aquinas to Tillich, plump for something in the (4) – (6) range and explicitly reject (1). The possibility of (3) has been almost wholly ignored, and (2) has not fared much better.' Whatever we call the category, (3) is something for which we have already argued above. Alston himself particularly wants to defend (2).

His main argument, contrary to Aquinas' position (although compare Swinburne, 1977, chapter 5), is that it is possible to apply many human terms univocally to God, at least in a modified way, because some human terms ('know', 'will', 'love', 'forgive', 'make', etc.) retain a 'common core of meaning' when they are applied to God. For example:

What it is for God to *make something* is radically different from what it is for a human being to make something; but that does not rule out an abstract feature in common, for example, *that by the exercise of agency something comes into existence.* (p. 24)

Alston encourages us to adopt a *functionalist* analysis of human psychological concepts. Such terms, he contends, carry no implications about the structure or ontology of the human mind or brain, but rather point to a particular function or 'job'. When they are applied to God, therefore, they can point to the same function, but without implying the limitations that they have when applied to us creatures. That is, the *functional concept* is the same, although its 'realisation' is very different in God, on the one hand, and human beings, on the other.

Richard Swinburne comes to the similar conclusion that 'wise', 'powerful' and 'good' are univocal in their use of us and God, and are not employed in any special theological sense. Thus 'wise' is still synonymous with 'knows many things' and contrary to 'foolish', although 'there are differences in what wisdom amounts to in God' (Swinburne, 1992, p. 152, cf. p. 37). But he argues that other predicates, such as 'sees', 'feels pity/anger' and 'loves', have to be used analogically of God because they normally imply bodily sensations or desires.

EXERCISE

Re-read Alston's argument and see if you can analyse other terms in the way he proposes, as applying 'with a single voice' to both ourselves and God. (To begin with, you might try 'forgives'.) Are you convinced that some words can be applied (almost?) univocally to God?

Can the argument be extended to 'lives'? What about 'exists'?

Further reading

Davies, B (1985), *Thinking about God*, London, Chapman, chapter 5.

Davies, B (1993), *An Introduction to the Philosophy of Religion*, Oxford, Oxford University Press, chapter 2.

Fawcett, T (1970), *The Symbolic Language of Religion*, London, SCM, chapter 4.

Mascall, E L (1966), *Existence and Analogy*, London, Darton, Longman and Todd.

Mitchell, B (1990), *How to Play Theological Ping-Pong: and other essays on faith and reason*, Grand Rapids, Michigan, Eerdmans, chapter 12.

Owen, H P (1969), *The Christian Knowledge of God*, London, Athlone, chapters 9 and 10.

Ross, J (1998), Religious language, in B Davies (ed.), *Philosophy of Religion: a guide to the subject*, pp. 106–135, London, Cassell.

Soskice, J M (1985), *Metaphor and Religious Language*, Oxford, Oxford University Press, pp. 64–66.

Stiver, D R (1996), *The Philosophy of Religious Language: sign, symbol, and story*, Oxford, Blackwell, pp. 23–29, 124–127.

Ward, K (1996), *Religion and Creation*, Oxford, Oxford University Press, chapter 6.

6. LANGUAGES AT WAR

Introduction

People regularly use a variety of forms of language when speaking of the same topic without generating any sense of unease or conflict in themselves or those who listen to them. So someone might ask you about, say, a parent or friend, and given long enough – and sufficient interest from your questioner – you may find yourself describing:

- their appearance, age and health;
- their other relationships;
- their paid employment (if any);
- their personality and character;
- their interests, hobbies and pastimes;
- their opinions and values.

Such forms of discourse may be said to be *complementary* (which means, of course, that they 'go together', not that they are involved in mutual back-slapping!).

But when the subject-matter changes, some forms of language can appear to clash. This is particularly the case when religious matters are under consideration.

Reflecting on experience
Think of a religious topic of significance to you that gives rise to controversy because it is described in one sort of discourse (such as history or one of the sciences) in a way that seems to conflict with its religious meaning and interpretation.

How do you deal with such conflicts?

In the field of religion there are many such examples of languages at war. They include the miracle stories from the Bible and religious tradition for which people have offered 'scientific' or common-sense, non-miraculous explanations. For example, some have suggested that the manna described in Exodus 16:4–21 was a type of honeydew excreted by insects, and others that the feeding of the five thousand in Mark 6:30–44 was the result of people sharing their own food in response to one boy's generosity. Similarly, the scientific (or common-sense) story of what happens to a body after death is in conflict with the biblical story of the raising of Lazarus (John 11), the resurrection of Jesus himself and at least some general beliefs about life after death.

In the above examples (broadly) *scientific* language is in a state of apparent conflict with religious or theological claims. Other examples might come to mind where it is *history* that seems to be in conflict with religion. For example, an historical account of the Israelites' Exodus from Egypt, their conquest and possession of the 'promised land', and their subsequent Exile from it and return from Exile will locate these facts in a secular story about tribal wars and migrations and the territorial ambitions of empires. By contrast, the accounts in the prophetic and historical books of the Old Testament speak of God's action in history and the way God's plan is fulfilled through the behaviour of other nations (see, for example, 2 Samuel 22; 2 Kings 6:32 to 7:8; Amos 6; Isaiah 43:14–21 and 45:1–7). Like the scientists, the historians will not mention God in their stories at all.

To put it at its most basic level, religious discourse describes certain events in history and human biography using such terms as the 'plan of God' or 'acts of God', the divine 'necessity', 'providence', 'grace', and so on. The *same* events, situation or phenomena may be described in very different language, however, using the vocabulary of 'chance', 'laws of Nature', or 'human potential' and political activity. Can they both be right, or is religious discourse *undermined* by this alternative, secular way of speaking?

For many people, the languages of history and of science are greatly to be preferred over the language of religion or theology for one main reason: the different relationships they have to evidence. Historical and scientific assertions can and must be tested against the evidence; their claims are public and verifiable. The case of God-talk, however, seems to be very different. Is evidence at all relevant here; is it ever appealed to? Don't religious people pride themselves in believing *despite the evidence*?

Meaning and evidence

In the middle of the last century this clash of languages gave rise to an intense debate about the 'meaningfulness' of religious language. It originated in a short-lived philosophical movement called logical positivism, which sought to limit all real knowledge to propositions that were either true by definition (e.g. 'all triangles have three angles') or could be verified, at least in principle, by human sense experience. Religious (and moral) claims, because they fell into neither category, tended to be dismissed as 'meaningless', as having no cognitive (factual) meaning. Such claims could only serve to express the speaker's emotions; they possessed what was sometimes described as 'emotive meaning'. 'A sentence is factually significant to any given person, if, and only if, he knows how to verify the proposition which it purports to express' (Ayer, 1946, p. 35). In other words, it has meaning only if sense experience would be able to decide its truth.

Why was this debate ever joined? Why worry about testing whether language has meaning? Well, although no one is likely ever to ask, it would be very easy to answer the question, 'What do you mean by saying that there is a cat [or a two-headed, pink unicorn] in the next room?' The answer is something like this: 'If I were to go into the next room and look, I should discover a cat [unicorn].' 'Julius Caesar had a hooked nose' is similarly testable, even though I cannot myself test it in such a direct way (but Caesar's companions could).

But what about: 'Everything in the universe has just doubled in size, as has the speed of light'? Isn't that impossible to test, since all our rulers have grown to the same extent as the things they measure? Or try these: 'There is a bodiless spirit in the next room'; 'There is a leprechaun in my sock drawer'; 'The square roots are ecstatic this morning, and Absolute Being changeth not.' At some point someone is likely to cry, 'Nonsense!' – that is, 'none sense': 'that claim makes (has) no sense (or meaning).' It is meaningless; there is nothing that it means.

Note that even false propositions have meaning; but meaningless propositions cannot be either true or false, for they say nothing. Note too that, in this context, *meaningfulness* is used as a term that labels sentences or phrases, or (better) the propositions they express, rather than experiences, situations or lives. If a logical positivist says that some utterance is meaningful, he is not saying that it is deep, or that it engenders a sense of purpose or value. He just means that it asserts or implies or denies something; it 'makes sense'.

We do think like this about a lot of claims; and we often dismiss another person's talk as meaningless if we cannot imagine how the truth of his claim could ever be tested.

EXERCISE

Consider the following propositions:

(a) 'In order to understand a statement, we must know what the world (or, more broadly, "reality") would be like if it were true.'

(b) 'A sentence only has meaning if you know how to check whether it is true or false.'

Do you agree with either proposition? Are they saying the same thing? What implications might they have for religious utterances?

The challenge of falsification

Logical positivism soon died out, partly because its own 'verification principle' declared itself meaningless (as it was itself neither a tautology nor verifiable by sense experience)! But it left its mark in the form of a heightened concern both for the meaning of language, and for linking that meaning with issues of truth and evidence, and this proved to be very influential in discussions about religious language. The criterion most often cited in that debate was that a proposition is factually meaningful only if it is in principle *falsifiable* by human sense experience. That is to say, a form of words can only be said really to state something if we know what evidence would show it to be false.

The humanist philosopher Antony Flew famously applied this *Falsification Challenge* to theology. He argued that as a theological claim did not really deny anything, it did not assert anything either, and therefore that 'it is not really an assertion'. If religious talk could not show itself to be *open to falsification*, it would have to be rejected as having no meaning.

There are several aspects to this challenge that we should notice right away.

• Flew's criterion (which itself is not falsifiable) was little more than a restatement of the positivist's assumption that all cognitive language needs to be open to testing by sense experience. Meaning is still said to be dependent on evidence. Nevertheless, it has made certain features of the meaning of religious language clear and has provoked some interesting rejoinders.

- It is easier to specify what sort of experience would falsify a claim than it is to say what would verify it. (Thus the evidence of one black swan falsifies the claim that 'all swans are white', a claim that would take for ever to verify.) The phrase 'in principle' also allows us to make meaningful claims that *in practice* are not open to empirical falsification – for example, scientific claims about events long ago or on distant galaxies that generate no evidence that is observable to us.

- The philosopher of science Karl Popper used a falsifiability criterion to distinguish scientific (or 'empirical') claims, which were open to falsification, from other sorts of claim that were not. For him, however, this was only a criterion of demarcation, useful for separating science from other subjects.

- Religious believers face many criticisms, including the challenge to justify the *truth* of their statements. Flew's challenge is prior even to this, and picks up the sceptic's question (or the child's question): 'What does it *mean* to say that God loves us, or that God exists?' Flew links the two challenges, so that the answer to the question, 'How do you know that this is true?' is made to determine the answer to the question, 'What does it mean?'

The parable of the gardener

Flew argued that theology's assertions are always qualified in such a way and to such an extent that they can never be shown to be false. But in protecting itself in this way, theology's 'fine, brash hypothesis' about God's relationship to the world dies 'the death of a thousand qualifications', showing that it had no real factual meaning in the first place.

EXERCISE

📖 Read and reflect on the passage from Flew printed below.

How serious a challenge is this? How might the religious believer respond to it?

Once upon a time two explorers came upon a clearing in the jungle. In the clearing were growing many flowers and many weeds. One explorer says, 'Some gardener must tend this plot.' The other disagrees, 'There is no gardener.' So they pitch their tents and set a watch. No gardener is ever seen. 'But perhaps he is an invisible gardener.' So they set up a barbed-wire fence. They electrify it. They patrol with bloodhounds . . . But no shrieks ever suggest that some intruder has received a shock. No movements of the wire ever betray an invisible climber. The blood-hounds never give cry. Yet still the Believer is not convinced. 'But there is a gardener, invisible, intangible, insensible to electric shocks, a gardener who has no scent and makes no sound, a gardener who comes secretly to look after the garden which he loves.' At last the Sceptic despairs, 'But what remains of your original assertion? Just how does what you call an invisible, intangible, eternally elusive gardener differ from an imaginary gardener or even from no gardener at all?'

In this parable we can see how what starts as an assertion, that something exists or that there is some analogy between certain complexes of phenomena, may be reduced step by step to an altogether different status, to an expression perhaps of a 'picture preference'. The Sceptic says there is no gardener. The Believer says there is a gardener (but invisible, etc.). . . . But though the process of qualification may be, and of course usually is, checked in time, it is not always judiciously so halted. Someone may dissipate his assertion completely without noticing that he has done so. . . .

When the Sceptic in the parable asked the Believer, 'Just how does what you call an invisible, intangible, eternally elusive gardener differ from an imaginary gardener or even from no gardener at all?' he was suggesting that the Believer's earlier statement had been so eroded by qualification that it was no longer an assertion at all. (Flew and Mac-Intyre, 1955, pp. 96–98)

Scholars have summarised the value of Flew's challenge under several headings.
- It shows that the claim that the world is a sort of garden that requires a sort of gardener is *not* an empirically-testable hypothesis; or at any rate it shows that God is not open to direct empirical observation, so that whatever people mean by 'finding' or 'experiencing' God is very different from what they usually mean by using these words.
- It identifies serious challenges to religious claims about God's providential care that are posed by the lack of unambiguous evidence. It

therefore raises the problem of evil in a stark manner. Later in his essay Flew asks what would have to happen for believers to deny that God loves us as a father does, citing the example of a child dying of inoperable throat cancer.

- It challenges believers to give their religious language content by saying what sort of difference it would make if it were true.

Philosophers of religion have offered an interesting range of responses to this challenge, a number of which were also couched in parabolic form.

Escaping the challenge: non-cognitive responses

A non-cognitive interpretation of religious beliefs treats them as expressions of feelings, emotions or attitudes to life, or of commitments to a certain way of behaving. On this view, rather than imparting information, religious language arouses and deepens attitudes and emotions, and stirs people to moral and religious action. It also evokes, fosters and clarifies our experiences and interpretations of Nature and human life. What it does not do, however, is make any claims that can be true or false about God or 'another world' (or about this world, come to that). Religious belief is therefore not a type of factual belief, and religious language has no cognitive (fact-asserting) function. Those who take this non-cognitive view could happily accept the empiricists' criterion of meaningfulness for factual claims (although not all do), while insisting that as religious language does not have factual meaning, the criterion does not apply in this area.

The philosopher Richard Braithwaite described our religious and moral beliefs as declarations of policies about behaviour. Braithwaite recognised that moral statements have a meaning, despite the fact that they are not empirically testable. He said that they express or show forth, but do not make statements about, attitudes; moral assertions work by declaring an intention (see Chapter 8 below). Religious assertions should be interpreted in much the same way: the 'primary use of religious assertions is to announce allegiance to a set of moral principles'; they are declarations of commitment to a certain way of life (Braithwaite, 1966, p. 63). 'God is love' is therefore to be understood non-cognitively, as ' I intend to live a loving life.' While this may be associated with certain religious stories or myths, these are only there to inspire us psychologically; we do not need to believe that they are true.

EXERCISE

How convincing is this account? Is this how religious people
use religious language?

Braithwaite is correct that religious assertions often function as
expressions of attitudes and commitments. But surely religion *also*
makes cognitive claims (either directly or by implication) about God's
nature, Jesus' resurrection, the prophetic status of Muhammad, and so
on. Can religion be entirely collapsed into morality? (Others would
argue that moral statements also make factual claims.)

Richard Hare held a similar view to Braithwaite's (see Hare, 1992, pp.
1–36). His particular notoriety derives from his suggestion (in Flew and
MacIntyre, 1955, pp. 99–103) that religious belief might be on a par with
the paranoid student's view that all his lecturers are out to murder him.
Both, Hare argues, are *unverifiable and unfalsifiable interpretations of
experience*, which shape and direct our view of reality. Everyone has such
bliks (Hare's word). According to Hare, they are certainly meaningful
and may be sane (reasonable?) or deluded. He allows that the student's
blik is 'insane'; the view that the world will hold together, however, is a
sane blik.

But what about the view that the world is created by a good God? The
point here is that these broad interpretations of experience are constructed to take account of contrary evidence, so that such evidence is
never going to falsify them. I might insist, 'Lecturer A was nice to me
today – but that just shows how cunning he is'; similarly, 'The floor-
boards seem a bit wonky, but it is only the loose nails – it is not that the
laws of Nature have ceased to hold this morning.'

More recently, post-modernist thinkers such as John Caputo and Don
Cupitt have embraced what they take to be the original and authentic
understanding of religious truth, interpreting it as 'a truth without
Knowledge . . . a *deed*, not a thought, something that demands our
response', it is a truth that we must make *happen* (Caputo, 2001, p. 115).
For Cupitt too, religious truth is practical and subjective, and God is
explicitly defined as a symbol or personified ideal, a 'humanly-needed
way of speaking generated by the impact of the religious demand and
ideal upon us' (Cupitt, 1980, p. 133). Such accounts immunise religion
from the Falsification Challenge, by adopting some form of theological

non-realism (the belief that God only exists as an idea, a human creation).

Rising to the challenge: cognitive responses

Other writers have continued to accept that religious language does assert facts about reality, that is, that it is cognitive. A number have also expressed at least a qualified acceptance of the criterion of meaning for factual claims proposed by Flew and other 'logical empiricists', while arguing that although theological assertions are falsifiable (or verifiable, or at least 'checkable') *in principle* by human sense experience, their truth or falsity cannot always *in practice* be determined – at least, not in this life.

The parable of the stranger

Basil Mitchell offered this as a better account of the religious life than that of Flew's absent gardener. Mitchell argued that the believer (or 'theologian') does not, in fact, deny that evidence counts against his assertions. For example, she or he would recognise that the existence of pain and suffering does count against Christian doctrine. 'But it is true that he will not allow it – or anything – to count decisively against it; for he is committed by his faith to trust in God. His attitude is not that of the detached observer, but of the believer.' This is an example of *trust*.

> In time of war in an occupied country, a member of the resistance meets one night a stranger who deeply impresses him. They spend that night together in conversation. The Stranger tells the partisan that he himself is on the side of the resistance – indeed that he is in command of it, and urges the partisan to have faith in him no matter what happens. The partisan is utterly convinced at that meeting of the Stranger's sincerity and constancy and undertakes to trust him.
>
> They never meet in conditions of intimacy again. But sometimes the Stranger is seen helping members of the resistance, and the partisan is grateful and says to his friends, 'He is on our side.'
>
> Sometimes he is seen in the uniform of the police handing over patriots to the occupying power. On these occasions his friends murmur against him: but the partisan still says 'He is on our side.' He still believes that, in spite of appearances, the Stranger did not deceive him. Sometimes he asks the Stranger for help and receives it. He is then thankful. Sometimes he asks and does not receive it. Then he says, 'The

Stranger knows best.' Sometimes his friends, in exasperation, say 'Well, what *would* he have to do for you to admit that you were wrong and that he is not on our side?' But the partisan refuses to answer. He will not consent to put the Stranger to the test . . .

The partisan of the parable does not allow anything to count decisively against the proposition 'The Stranger is on our side.' This is because he has committed himself to trust the Stranger. But he of course recognizes that the Stranger's ambiguous behaviour *does* count against what he believes about him. It is precisely this situation which constitutes the trial of his faith. (Mitchell, in Flew and MacIntyre, 1955, pp. 103–104)

EXERCISE

How do you respond to Mitchell's parable?

How good is it as a portrayal of the nature of religious faith, and how relevant is it to Flew's challenge?

Mitchell may be said to have exposed some of the limitations of Flew's criterion of meaningfulness. But should this picture of the believer satisfy Flew? In Mitchell's parable, evidence is now relevant to religious claims, but never decisively so; God is let off the hook yet again. But Mitchell seems to be correct in admitting that in theory religious belief can be falsified, while implying that in practice we cannot predict when – or whether – this will happen for any given believer. Belief is, after all, *someone's* belief, and whether I carry on trusting an ambiguous God is going to be a personal judgement. No computer algorithm can do it for me, even if it has access to all the data; it is *believers* who believe. Some will give up their faith quickly; others will stick at it for a lifetime (see Mark 4:1–20).

Other philosophers have expressed a position similar to that of Mitchell, by drawing parallels between the problem of justifying religious belief and the difficulty of knowing whether someone loves us, or of justifying our own love. Neither is just about feelings, nor is it simply non-rational, for we can point to reasons for loving and for trusting another's love. But our reasons for loving someone are individual, personal reasons, which would not necessarily count for others. And our belief in another's love shouldn't just crumble (be 'falsified') at our first row, and can only be tested (and 'verified'?) against a lifetime's experience.

> The test of whether our 'falling in love' is or is not reasonable will be . . . whether the resulting loyalty and pro-attitude can remain when confronted with a larger and larger picture. (Ramsey, 1964a, p. 214; see also 1964b, p. 38)

But, of course, trusting strangers and lovers is very different from trusting God. After all, we have unambiguous empirical evidence of their existence, but not of God's. The believer may say that she has 'met' God, but is that an empirically verifiable species of meeting? (See Chapters 2 and 3.)

The parable of the road

This is John Hick's way of presenting the idea that, while religious claims cannot be proved to be true in this life, they could be verified in an after-life. (Interestingly, on this account verification is possible but *falsification* is not, for if there is no after-life we shall never come to know that our religious beliefs are false.)

> Two men are travelling together along a road. One of them believes that it leads to a Celestial City, the other that it leads nowhere; but since this is the only road there is, both must travel it. Neither has been this way before, and therefore neither is able to say what they will find around each next corner. During their journey they meet both with moments of refreshment and delight, and with moments of hardship and danger. All the time one of them thinks of his journey as a pilgrimage to the Celestial City and interprets the pleasant parts as encouragements and the obstacles as trials of his purpose and lessons in endurance, prepared by the king of that city and designed to make of him a worthy citizen of the place when at last he arrives there. The other, however, believes none of this and sees their journey as an unavoidable and aimless ramble. Since he has no choice in the matter, he enjoys the good and endures the bad. But for him there is no Celestial City to be reached, no all-encompassing purpose ordaining their journey, only the road itself and the luck of the road in good weather and in bad.
>
> During the course of the journey the issue between them is not an experimental one. They do not entertain different expectations about the coming details of the road, but only about its ultimate destination.

And yet when they do turn the last corner it will be apparent that one of them has been right all the time and the other wrong. Thus although the issue between them has not been experimental, it has nevertheless from the start been a real issue. They have not merely felt differently about the road; for one was feeling appropriately and the other inappropriately in relation to the actual state of affairs. Their opposed interpretations of the road constituted genuinely rival assertions, though assertions whose assertion-status has the peculiar characteristic of being guaranteed retrospectively by a future crux. (Hick, in Mitchell, 1971, pp. 59–60)

Hick called this *eschatological verification* (eschatology is the doctrine of the last things – including death, judgement and heaven). Put briefly, his point is that if in heaven there is sufficiently convincing evidence that we have 'arrived', then the belief that the road leads there may be said to be a meaningful belief. It can be said to have factual meaning *now*, on the grounds that (for some, at least) there will be something that can show it to be true in the future.

EXERCISE

Ian Crombie published an earlier paper that hinted at a similar solution. He raised a number of questions (in Flew and MacIntyre, 1955, p. 124). How might Hick answer them?
(a) Does anything count against the assertion that God is merciful?
(b) Does anything count decisively against it?
(c) Could anything count decisively against it?
(d) Can we design a crucial experiment? If so, what would it be? If not, why not?

Here are Crombie's responses to his own questions:
(a) Yes, suffering.
(b) No, because it is true.
(c) Yes, 'suffering which was utterly, eternally and irredeemably pointless'.
(d) No, because we can never see all of the picture. 'Two things at least are hidden from us; what goes on in the recesses of the personality of the sufferer, and what shall happen hereafter.'

Certainly, there is no knock-down, unambiguous evidence for the truth of religious belief one way or another *in this life*. As for the world to come, will that be any less ambiguous? Hick has offered a theoretical sense in which religious claims can be said to be empirically verifiable, but we might ask just how 'empirical' is an experience after death? (It is not going to be sense experience as we know it, Captain.)

Dismissing the challenge

Other philosophers of religion have resisted the Falsifiability Challenge in a more radical fashion.

Both Hick and Mitchell appeal to a form of experience that isn't quite the normal, everyday sense of experience that the unbeliever in Flew's parable is looking for. Can we push at this open door? You may agree with Flew that the meaning of language about facts is linked with evidence in such a way that we cannot have the former without some appeal to the latter. But why not broaden the notion of evidence to include 'moral experience' and even 'religious experience'? We might be able to defend these forms of ('non-sensuous') experience as providing evidence of the truth, and therefore of the meaningfulness, of moral and religious claims. This approach rejects outright the limitation of experience to sense experience in Flew's challenge, interpreting this as a narrow criterion of *empiricality* rather than a broad criterion of *meaningfulness*.

An even shorter way with the falsifiability/verifiability criterion is to declare that it simply confuses the *meaning* of a statement, what philosophers call its 'truth conditions' – the conditions under which it would be true – with the *evidence* for it, what we might call its 'checking conditions' – the conditions under which *we would know* that it is true. Can we not distinguish between what a statement asserts, what it means, and the evidence for its truth? If we can, then we can argue that a sentence has cognitive (factual) meaning if it asserts or denies that something is the case. On this account, it is not necessary that any of the claims that it entails or denies are expressed in ways that can be checked against *any* sort of evidence or experience. A sentence is meaningful if its words are used according to the rules or practice of a language. *That is all that is needed*. (See Heimbeck, 1969, chapter II.)

Further reading

Clack, B and Clack, B R (1998), *The Philosophy of Religion: a critical introduction*, Cambridge, Polity, pp. 81–109.

Ferré, F (1962), *Language, Logic and God*, London, Eyre and Spottiswoode, chapters 3 and 4.

Gill, J H (1976), *Ian Ramsey: to speak responsibly of God*, London, George Allen and Unwin, chapters 1 and 2.

Hick, J (1990), *Philosophy of Religion*, Englewood Cliffs, New Jersey, Prentice-Hall, chapters 7 and 8.

Hordern, W (1964), *Speaking of God: the nature and purpose of theological language*, London, Epworth.

Nielsen, K (1982), *An Introduction to the Philosophy of Religion*, London, Macmillan, chapter 6.

Pailin, D A (1986), *Groundwork of Philosophy of Religion*, London, Epworth, chapter 11.

Stiver, D R (1996), *The Philosophy of Religious Language: sign, symbol and story*, Oxford, Blackwell, chapters 3 and 4.

Tilley, T W (1978), *Talking of God: an introduction to philosophical analysis of religious language*, New York, Paulist, chapters 1, 2 and 5.

7. RELIGIOUS LANGUAGE IN RELIGIOUS LIFE

Introduction

Whenever I take a journey that involves driving on the M6, I turn off towards the town where I was born and brought up, in order to place some flowers on the family grave. Why? I do not believe that my parents or grandparents know about this action, nor even whether, if they did, they would approve.

If a friend or relative is unwell or in some other kind of need, or is facing a difficult decision or situation, I often go into a church or cathedral and 'light a candle for her'. Why? I do not imagine that I am engaged in giving a gift to God (a gift of what – light?) or trying to catch God's attention. I might tell my friend what I intend to do or what I have done, but mostly I don't.

So why do I do such things? Probably because they *can* be done; they are things that I can *do*. I suppose that they are like little private religious rituals. And religious rituals, which represent a sub-set of religious activity, can be very important in our lives. I would feel bad about driving past the turn off to my home town, or neglecting to take the time to light that candle.

Reflecting on experience
Try to think of all the different *actions* that people engage in – including yourself? – that could broadly be described as 'religious'. Don't just confine your list to explicitly religious actions and practices such as kneeling to pray, crossing yourself, exchanging the 'Peace' at the Eucharist, going on pilgrimages, and so on. Think as well about smaller rituals or pieces of behaviour that are not so obviously expressions of commitments, values or beliefs (like putting flowers on a grave).

Students of the place of religion in society often draw attention to the widespread phenomenon of 'folk religion' or 'common religion'. These terms label a motley collection of attitudes, beliefs, values and *behaviour* that lie outside the control of religious institutions (unlike 'conventional religion'). Folk religion has been designated 'the underlife of religion' (Clark, 1982, p. viii) and comes to expression among churchgoers as well as those who never attend. It also merges with attitudes, beliefs and practices that have a less overtly supernatural reference, but which nonetheless fulfil functions that are similar to those of official or overt religion, in expressing people's deeply held values and their sense that life has a purpose. This last category has been variously described as 'invisible', 'surrogate' or 'implicit religion' (Luckmann, 1967; Bailey, 1997). Examples might include the convictions, values and rituals that undergird our friendships and family life; our membership of a school, college or club; or our passionate support for a team (or even, as Bailey suggests, going to the pub!).

Widening the discussion in this way shows us that it is very difficult to draw a line between what is religious and what is not, particularly if we focus on the place that certain activities have in people's lives, and compare these activities with the more explicitly religious practices endorsed by the Christian Church or by other religious bodies.

Finding forms of life

EXERCISE
Having reflected on your experience of religious action, try now to list the range of *religious behaviour* (or quasi-religious behaviour) that you came up with. Then ask yourself whether there are any particular types of *religious language* that are associated with each of these different activities.

Add to your list some examples of the sorts of things people say to and about God in these different contexts.

In his later period, the philosopher Ludwig Wittgenstein claimed that 'the *speaking* of language is part of an activity, or of a form of life', and that 'to imagine a language means to imagine a form of life' (1968, §§23,

19). Even more mysteriously, he wrote: 'what has to be accepted, the given, is – so one could say – *forms of life*' (1968, p. 226).

There is much dispute about what Wittgenstein meant by this phrase. Some scholars (including his pupil Norman Malcolm) take form of life to mean a way of life, and regard religion itself as a prime example. This is unlikely; most probably what Wittgenstein had in mind was something at once more limited and more natural, even biological: that is, instinctive human tendencies that are influenced by and expressed in culture (Clack, 1999, pp. 88–89). What cannot be in doubt is Wittgenstein's insistence that all language is rooted within human activity, including pre-rational action; it is 'an extension of primitive behaviour' (Wittgenstein, 1967, §545). For Wittgenstein, ritual actions and ceremonies, like the ones I confessed to at the beginning of this chapter, are not so much the product of careful reasoning and consideration of consequences, but represent an acting out of a more-or-less natural instinct (Clack, 1999, chapter 5).

In Wittgenstein's eyes, action always comes first and is the context in which our language makes sense. Quoting Goethe, he insists that 'in the beginning was the deed' (1980, p. 31). And yet Wittgenstein is often cited as an energetic hand on the steering wheel of 'the linguistic turn' in philosophy, theology and general intellectual reflection. How can this be?

Playing language games

Interestingly, this same Wittgenstein had earlier published a seminal work (known as the *Tractatus*), which argued that language needs to *picture* facts in the world, in the way that a drawing of a road accident represents the facts about the relationship between real cars. This way of analysing language was very influential among the logical positivists, whose effect on religious discourse we observed in the last chapter. Having published this book Wittgenstein believed that he had solved all the major problems of philosophy and he gave it up altogether for a period. Eventually, however, he returned to Cambridge and began developing a very different approach to language. This new account wasn't dominated by simple description, but focused instead on the vast range of *uses* associated with language. The functions of words, he now claimed, are as diverse as the functions of all the different tools in a toolbox (1968, §§11–15). Wittgenstein now insisted that 'the meaning of a word is its use in the language' (§43).

Here is another homely example that Wittgenstein employed: learning to use language is like discovering how to play a game by learning the rules (the logical 'grammar'). There is no suggestion here that this is 'just playing' and not a wholly serious matter. Wittgenstein only intends to make clear that philosophy, instead of legislating as to what the rules of any such *language game* should be like, ought to go out into the world – back to the 'rough ground' of real language (1968, §107) – in order to see how we really live our lives, how people in fact talk, and what language games are actually played. 'Only in the stream of thought and life do words have meaning', he wrote (1967, §173). Out there, in the real world, the philosopher will discover that there are a lot of different language games being played.

Wittgenstein's examples of language games are quite specific. They include 'reporting an event', 'giving orders', 'play-acting', 'making a joke', and 'asking, thanking, greeting, praying' (1968, §23). Although some have spoken broadly of religion itself as a whole language game, it is more sensible to think of religious talk as made up of a number of smaller religious language *games*, each with different rules and therefore with different criteria for 'making a mistake'. Many of these games are very different from many of the language games that we find within science and history. Therefore the way that we justify our use of religious language needs to be very different from the way that we justify our use of scientific or historical language. The challenges to the meaningfulness of *religious* language that we looked at in the last chapter, however, treated it as if it were bound by the same empirical rules.

So Wittgenstein can be thought of as opening another door onto the room where religious language is locked in combat with the Falsification Challenge, through which religion can escape unharmed.

EXERCISE

Do religious people treat their deepest religious beliefs and activities as if they were like scientific or historical hypotheses and procedures which have to be tested against empirical evidence?

Reflect on some concrete examples. How do we find out whether 'prayer is valid' or that 'the sacraments bestow grace'? How do people 'discern the Spirit'?

Back to the deed

For Wittgenstein, a language game consists of 'language and the actions into which it is woven' (1968, §7). Language games only exist *within* forms of life. We noted above that these might be thought of as instinctive actions, but such actions might also develop into practices and institutions, even cultures. Despite his focus on language, therefore, Wittgenstein insisted that language must be seen not just as a form of words, but in terms of the contextualised, public use that is made of those words. 'Our talk gets its meaning from the rest of our proceedings' (Wittgenstein, 1974, §229).

> Language is a characteristic part of a large group of activities – talking, writing, travelling on a bus, meeting a man, etc. We are concentrating [in analysing expressions of approval], not on the words 'good' or 'beautiful', . . . but on the occasions on which they are said . . . We don't start from certain words, but from certain occasions or activities.
>
> (Wittgenstein, 1966, p. 2)

Whatever these forms of life are, they are the *givens* – this is what people do. All justification 'comes to an end', Wittgenstein argued, not in our seeing a proposition to be true, but in relating it to human action: 'it is our *acting*, which lies at the bottom of our language-game' (1974, p. 204). The profound implication of this for religion is that *the meaning of religious belief is grounded in religious behaviour*.

EXERCISE

What do you make of this claim for the importance of locating religious language and religious belief in the context of religious action?

How might this affect the way that we think about religious language?

Wittgenstein privileged working religious language, which is set in the context of religious conduct and religious experience, over second-order, intellectualised theological theory. He contended, for example, that predestination is 'less a theory than a sigh, or a cry', for in analysing religious words what matters is 'the difference they make at various points in your life': '*practice* gives the words their sense' (Wittgenstein, 1980, pp. 30, 85). Paradoxically, then, despite his focus on language, Wittgenstein's view of religious belief – which was that of a sympathetic unbeliever (Clack, 1999, pp. 124–129) – was of something that was:

> shown by what we do rather than by what we say, in *praxis* rather than in dogma, theory and theological speculation. And, of course, it is shown in our attitudes, which are a part of *praxis*. (Barrett, 1991, p. 208)

In order to understand people's religious beliefs, therefore, we must observe the forms of life of – or within – their religion. Hence, when confronted by religious talk and especially if we are tempted to accuse it of confusion, 'what we need is not to look at the sentence, but at what [they] do with it . . . we must not think – impose our *a priori* assumptions – but look' (Phillips, 1993, p. 115; cf. Wittgenstein, 1968, §66). As Wittgenstein argued, we should not ask about meaning but about use. 'We actually have to *look* at how our language about God works, how it is used, if we are to get any real understanding of what it is [for example] for God to be a person, an agent' (Moore, 1988, p. 102). And that use includes looking at the religious life from within which it is spoken.

EXERCISE

Go back to Chapter 1 and review the distinction I made there between 'ordinary' and 'academic theology'. How would Wittgenstein respond to that analysis?

Wittgenstein's influence

The way that a number of scholars think about religious language has been profoundly influenced by what they take to be the insights of the later Wittgenstein. I shall mention just three examples here.

Fideism

Much discussion has centred on the work of those who seem to argue that Wittgenstein's reflections should encourage us to recognise the form of life and language game called religion as logically distinct from any other, and therefore immune from any criticisms that are based on criteria of meaning or truth derived from these other domains. This approach has been called *Wittgensteinian Fideism* (Nielsen, 1982, chapters 4 and 5) – 'fideism' being the view that religious knowledge rests on premises that must be accepted on faith and which cannot be established by rational means. It is said that if you adopt this position, certain claims follow:

- social life is compartmentalised into distinctive practices and languages that never interact (science, religion, witchcraft, etc.);
- only the insider (the believer who uses religious language) can understand religion; and
- because religious language and practice obviously exist and are long-established, they cannot be criticised as incoherent or untrue.

Dewi Phillips, who is often accused of adopting these positions, denies that they apply to him (Phillips, 1986). However, he is also insistent that religion is not a hypothesis about or a causal explanation of the world (as science is), but a way of seeing the world, 'a way of living, or a way of assessing life' (Wittgenstein, 1980, p. 64). He also holds that God's reality is not to be found *outside* religious practices and religious language, for 'to know how to use this language is to know God' (Phillips, 1965, p. 50), and it is religious discourse that tells us what is meant by 'God's reality':

> Coming to see that there is a God is not like coming to see that an additional being exists . . . Coming to see that there is a God involves seeing a new meaning in one's life, and being given a new understanding. (Phillips, 1967, p. 68)

Many think that Phillips' position sits too close to the overt non-realism, and related non-cognitivism, of people such as Cupitt (see Chapter 6), for whom 'belief in the God of Christian faith is an expression of allegiance to a particular set of values', a view that is said to derive from the recognition that 'the sense in which God is real is given in the language and practice of religion' (Cupitt, 1980, pp. 69, 57). Although he insists that 'God' is not the name of an individual, 'it does not refer to anything' (Phillips, 1976 p. 148), Phillips keeps closer to Wittgenstein in rejecting the general realism versus non-realism debate as a sterile example of language 'idling', instead of doing a proper job (thus Wittgenstein, 1967, §§ 413, 414; Phillips, 2001, p. 242). It is hard, however, not to interpret Phillips as a non-cognitivist in religion, and tempting to agree that 'in essence religious belief *is* religious activity for

Phillips'; it is (nothing more than) 'having a way of life' (Kellenberger, 1985, pp. 11, 32).

An area in which many readers may be more sympathetic to Phillips' Wittgensteinian approach is his emphasis on the *personal* nature of religious discourse. I take up this claim and its pastoral significance in the final chapter.

Post-liberalism

A currently highly influential understanding of theology that draws on many of Wittgenstein's concerns is *post-liberalism* (Lindbeck, 1984). George Lindbeck attacked liberal theology for locating the core of religion in common pre-reflective religious experience and existential concerns, thereby demoting the status of religion's external features – including its culture, tradition and language. By contrast, Lindbeck encourages us to adopt the view that the Christian religion is itself best understood as a cultural-linguistic system, with Christian doctrine providing the rules of the grammar of that religion: 'a religion can be viewed as a kind of cultural and/or linguistic framework or medium that shapes the entirety of life and thought.' On this account, religion is closely analogous to a language, and must be learned like a language is learned. To become a Christian is to acquire proficiency in the specific Christian language and form of life, which involves 'learning the story of Israel and of Jesus well enough to interpret and experience one's self and one's world in its terms' (pp. 33–34).

Lindbeck's account reduces doctrines to a regulative role, however, interpreting them not as statements but as *rules* (p. 19, cf. p. 107 and chapter 4). Unlike statements, rules cannot be judged either true or false. Now, this may be a useful analysis in the case of many doctrines. We could, for example, treat the doctrine of the Trinity as reminding us to follow the rule that, whenever we speak of God, we should use three sorts of language – Father-language, Son-language and Spirit-language. But even rules need some justification, and the usual justification for doctrinal rules is that they guide us in producing a theology that adequately represents the nature and activity of God.

Ordinary language theology

We have already met the post-modernist Christian theologian Don Cupitt. He follows Wittgenstein in taking a high view of ordinary language. In Cupitt's case, such language is perceived as 'the best radical theologian, and significantly sharper than the professionals', in that it embodies a vision of the human condition that is 'more substantial and even *formidable* than we have supposed' (Cupitt, 1999a, 'Foreword'; 1999b, p. 103). He argues that there is a philosophy of life built into our ordinary language that incorporates profound religious and moral ideas.

In his trilogy of books about the theology of everyday speech, Cupitt explores a range of everyday idioms, including references to 'life' and 'living'; and 'it', 'it all' and 'everything'. Much of this is not technically *God*-talk, which is not surprising as Cupitt draws his evidence not from religious believers but from common usage as described in dictionaries and collections of idioms, proverbs and slang. Nevertheless, in Cupitt's view this language certainly counts as *religious* discourse, even though it represents a very secular, relativist and non-realist spirituality. Cupitt's analysis may be thought of as broadening the categories of 'invisible', 'surrogate' and 'implicit' religion that we discussed above; it also suggests a wider range of linguistic accompaniments for the quasi-religious practices that we were thinking about at the beginning of this chapter.

See what you make of Cupitt's account of everyday religious speech (the idiomatic phrases are printed in **bold**).

> Mysteriously, nobody now seems to know any longer what it is or was *to love God*; but everyone seems to understand what it is **to love life**. In common speech and on the media we almost daily hear it said that all **life is sacred**; we hear talk of **the sanctity of life** and of **reverence** or **respect for life**, and we may hear quoted William Blake's '*Everything that lives is holy*': but when did you last hear the holiness or sacredness of *God* invoked seriously in everyday conversation? . . .
>
> What is religious, awesome and demanding about life is [the] combination of trembling contingency, evanescence, irrevocability, and infinite weight – neatly conveyed in idiomatic English by the question and answer: **Is this it? This is it**. Say those six words with stress on words two, three, four and six. That is the last truth. It's all there is to say. (Cupitt, 1999a, pp. 13, 86)

> **EXERCISE**
>
> Is there anything in these three ways of responding to
> Wittgenstein's work that seems to you to be particularly
> valuable for understanding religion?
>
> What criticisms would you make of these suggestions?

Further reading

Banner, M C (1990), *The Justification of Science and the Rationality of Religious Belief*, Oxford, Oxford University Press, chapter 4.

Clack, B R (1999), *An Introduction to Wittgenstein's Philosophy of Religion*, Edinburgh, Edinburgh University Press.

Clack, B and Clack, B R (1998), *The Philosophy of Religion: a critical introduction*, Cambridge, Polity, pp. 98–120.

Cupitt, D (1999), *The New Religion of Life in Everyday Speech*, London, SCM.

Cupitt, D (1999), *The Meaning of it All in Everyday Speech*, London, SCM.

Kerr, F (1997), *Theology after Wittgenstein*, London, SPCK.

Lindbeck, G A (1984), *The Nature of Doctrine: religion and theology in a postliberal age*, London, SPCK.

Moore, G (1988), *Believing in God: a philosophical essay*, Edinburgh, T and T Clark.

Phillips, D Z (1970), *Faith and Philosophical Enquiry*, London, Routledge and Kegan Paul.

Phillips, D Z (1993), *Wittgenstein and Religion*, Basingstoke, Macmillan.

Stiver, D R (1996), *The Philosophy of Religious Language: sign, symbol and story*, Oxford, Blackwell, chapter 6.

Wittgenstein, L (1966), *Lectures and Conversations on Aesthetics, Psychology and Religious Belief*, Oxford, Blackwell.

8. SPEAKING FOR OURSELVES

Introduction

The sub-title of this book is 'using language in religion'. This expresses one of its main objectives, which is to respond to the question, 'What use is religious language?'

This focus on the *use* of language marks something of a revolution in thinking about language among philosophers in the second half of the twentieth century. As we saw in the last chapter, Wittgenstein made an important contribution to this revolution by changing his own mind about what was most important about language. He encouraged others to stop asking what a particular form of words stands for or refers to, but to ask instead what the speaker or writer is employing it to *do* – what it is for, what functions it serves. This resulted in a new emphasis on analysing language as a tool for social interaction.

Reflecting on experience
Reflect on some of the things that you have said or written in the course of today, or have heard or read, paying particular attention to the different *uses* that are revealed in these pieces of (largely or wholly secular) language.

What was the speaker or writer trying to *do* with this language, and what *effects* did their language have on the listeners or hearers?

Speech as action

Language may be thought of as a form of action, a way in which people do things. Before applying this analysis to religious discourse, we need to explore in some detail what has come to be called the *speech act*, that is, the action that we perform in speaking or writing. Very obvious examples of speech acts that do things (other than stating or denying facts) are sometimes called 'performatives', which is an appropriate word. Think of performing the action of making a promise or a request, or expressing appreciation, or issuing an order. Even statements, however, are things that we do.

EXERCISE
On the following table, list as many examples as you can of the different functions that language can perform. It may be helpful to link an illustrative example with each category, as in the first two examples below.

TABLE 1

Language function	Example
• expressing an attitude	'You are disgusting.'
• making a request	'Please pass the salt.'
•	
•	
•	
•	
•	
•	

We shall return to the categorisation of the uses of language shortly, before trying to apply it to religious language.

J L Austin distinguished between three aspects, levels or dimensions of a speech act (Austin, 1962, pp. 95–107):

(a) the basic *locution* or 'locutionary act' *of* saying or writing something – that is, the utterance itself: what one actually says or writes;

(b) the *illocution* – that is, what is done *in* uttering these words: the kind of act that these words perform;

(c) the *perlocution* – that is, what is done *by* (is caused by) (a) and (b): the intended consequences of the speech act. Austin wrote:

Saying something will often . . . produce certain consequential effects upon the feelings, thoughts, or actions of the audience, or of the speaker, or of other persons: and it may be done with the design, intention or purpose of producing them. (Austin, 1962, p. 101)

This may all seem rather abstruse at the moment, but a couple of examples should help to make it clearer.

Example 1
If I say to you, 'Please open the door', my utterance can be analysed into three elements, along these lines:
(a) uttering the words, 'Please open the door' (locution); which issues
(b) a *request* (illocution); which has
(c) a causal *effect* (perlocution) on you, the hearer, by persuading you to open the door.

EXERCISE
You may like to try another example yourself. Analyse the more contentious expression, 'Shut your face', along similar lines.

Example 2
You might have identified the following three components:
(a) 'Shut your face' is said (locution);
(b) a *command* and an *insult* are issued, and certain *attitudes expressed* (all these are illocutions);
(c) a psychological or behavioural *effect* of some kind might be evoked in the hearer – perhaps he or she lapses into silence, or suffers a feeling of deflation. (This is the perlocutionary response.)

Note that element (b), the illocution, represents the *conventional aspect* of the utterance. This means that, provided the speaker is following the correct rules or conventions, her language cannot fail to have this illocutionary dimension. As long as they are said by the right people in the right circumstances, the following sentences will inevitably perform the deeds indicated in the right hand column of Table 2.

TABLE 2

Locution	Illocution
• 'I arrest you'	makes an arrest
• 'Beware of the bull' (on a notice)	issues a warning
• 'I baptise you in the name of the Father, and of the Son, and of the Holy Spirit'	performs a baptism

The conventional nature of illocutions is something that we rely on all the time in making promises, asking questions, and so on. However, element (c), the perlocution, is much less straightforward. This is the *causal aspect* of the speech act. Evoking the intended response doesn't just depend on the speaker or writer saying things properly. He or she may be using an appropriate conventional formula in order to insult someone, to get something done, or to encourage co-operation, but that will not always guarantee success. Everything depends on the effect of these well-chosen words on the listener or reader. Telling you to 'shut your face' probably will *not* coerce you into silence; it may instead provoke you into angry speech. If I evoke such an *unintended* response, my utterance can be said to have failed. Your response is still an *effect* of what I say, of course, but it could be argued that it cannot be an *act* of mine, at least if we specify that human 'acts' (or 'actions' or 'deeds') are intentional by definition. These non-intended effects of language are, however, very significant, as we shall see.

Things to do with words

We shall return to perlocutions later. At this point we need to concentrate on the variety of illocutions that may be carried out by different utterances, remembering that more than one illocution may be conveyed by the same speech act. For example, 'I believe in God' makes a statement, expresses a belief and perhaps also commits the speaker to certain actions. In the following analysis of illocutions I shall follow the classification of *four kinds of illocution* that is offered by the Dutch philosopher of religion Vincent Brümmer (Brümmer, 1981, chapter 2; cf. Austin, 1962, pp. 150–162). We may think of them as four basic *functions* that we can perform in speaking or writing language.

Constatives

Constatives make statements. We perform a constative when we assert that something is or is not the case through statements or assertions of various sorts – that is, when we affirm or deny a *proposition*. Unlike all other illocutions, constatives may be judged true or false. A philosopher would say, therefore, that the speech acts that contain them are *cognitive* (that is, 'factual' in the sense of asserting or denying facts). All the other types of illocution are *non-cognitive*, as they cannot be said to be either true or false. 'There is a cat on the mat' or 'There is a pink dinosaur up the chimney' is cognitive language ('factual', 'truth-claiming/denying', 'descriptive', 'either true or false'). But it does not make sense to ask whether a command, question, request or exclamation is true or false; hence, 'Go away' or 'Please help' or 'Are there any pink dinosaurs near here?' are all examples of non-cognitive language. These expressions have a meaning (a proper use) but it is not to assert that a certain state of affairs exists. They are neither true nor false.

This distinction between cognitive and non-cognitive uses of language is very important in religion, as we have already seen.

Expressives

*Expres*sives give expression to what the speaker feels or thinks. Utterances such as 'My soul thirsts for God' and 'I hate your views on women' contain an expressive element. Expressives may be expressions of attitudes or feelings (such as trust, longing, joy, wonder, dissatisfaction), but we can also express a conviction, a belief or an intention. Such expressions are non-cognitive. They are, however, often mistaken for cognitive speech acts, because it is easy to read them as *statements about* what I feel or believe. Autobiographical statements can indeed be true or false, but *expressions* of attitude, belief or intention are not the sort of thing that can be either true or false. People say such things not from a desire to inform us in a detached way about themselves, but to express what they feel, intend, believe, and so on.

> If a person says 'I feel bored', or 'I feel depressed', we do not ask him for his evidence, or request him to make sure. We may accuse him of shamming to us or to himself, but we do not accuse him of having been careless in his observations or rash in his inferences, since we do not think that his avowal was a report of observations or conclusions. He has not been a good or a bad detective; he has not been a detective at all . . . That is why, if we are suspicious, we do not ask 'fact or fiction?', 'true or false?', 'reliable or unreliable?', but 'sincere or shammed?' The conversational avowal of moods requires not acumen, but openness. It comes from the heart, not from the head. (Ryle, 1963, p. 102)

(To ask of a speech act whether it is sincere or insincere is quite a good way of showing that it contains or carries a non-cognitive expressive, just as asking whether it is true or false is a good test of whether it contains or carries a constative element.)

Commissives

*Commiss*ives are acts of commission or self-commitment. In a commissive a speaker commits herself or himself to some action and accepts an obligation to the hearer, by entering a contract, making a promise or taking a vow. It presupposes that such *speakers* are in the right position to do what they commit themselves to. Hence I cannot 'take you to be my wife' if I am already legally married, nor can I 'promise to grow an extra head during the night' (for even more obvious reasons). I cannot even promise to return your book unless I borrowed it in the first place. I must be capable of doing what I am committing myself to, but also capable of not doing it.

Prescriptives

*Prescript*ives prescribe what others should do. Through prescriptives I lay an obligation on my hearers to adopt a certain attitude or way of behaving. Commands, requests, offers of advice, and various formal phrases of appointment or judicial sentence contain illocutions of this kind. In these cases they presuppose that the *hearer* is in a position to do what is required, but also that she or he can refrain from doing so. I therefore cannot sensibly advise you to live for another two hundred years, or order you to discover a cure for the common cold or to stop feeling an emotion.

Sentences containing the word 'ought' contain prescriptives that prescribe *obligations*. These may be:

- unconditional *moral* obligations: for example, 'You ought to help refugees'; or
- conditional *non-moral* obligations: for example, 'You ought to study harder' [if you want to pass your exam], 'You shouldn't wear that hat' [if you don't want to look stupid].

Multi-tasking speech

Remember that any given speech act may convey more than one of these types of illocution. For example, like constatives, commissives are coupled with an expressive element: in committing myself to doing or not doing something and declaring myself answerable to my hearer(s) for fulfilling this commitment, I am at the same time expressing my *intention* of fulfilling my commitment. (Brümmer, 1981, p. 22)

Similarly, in requesting something of you I also express my wishes. Furthermore, other illocutions may be *implied by*, rather than *contained in* a speech act. In particular, a *constative* may be implied or presupposed by promises, requests, commitments, orders and offers of advice (Austin, 1970, p. 237). So 'Please open the door' implies that there is a door to be opened, and that it is currently shut. The factual implications of certain expressions will prove to be a very important issue in interpreting religious language, as we shall see.

Religious speech acts

We have been exploring how to do things with words quite generally. This can now serve as a basis for understanding some of the things that go on when we or others use *religious* language.

EXERCISE
You will find below a range of different religious utterances. It would be a useful exercise to classify them on the basis of the *main* actions or functions they perform, that is to say, the main illocutionary element (or 'load') that they carry – the one that characterises them as promises, statements or commands, or any of the actions we have just looked at.

To carry out this exercise, write the designated letter of each sentence against the appropriate illocutionary category ('constative', 'expressive', etc.) in Table 3 on pp. 96–97 below. (To start you off, I have already noted example (a) as being primarily characterised by an *expressive* function.)

(a) 'Holy, holy, holy Lord, God of power and might,
    heaven and earth are full of your glory.'
(b) 'The Lord is risen indeed, and he has appeared to Simon.'

(c) 'Go in peace to love and serve the Lord.'
(d) 'Take up your cross and follow Jesus.'
(e) 'I bind unto myself today the strong name of the Trinity.'
(f) 'O give thanks to the LORD; for he is good; for his steadfast love endures for ever.'
(g) 'As for me and my household, we will serve the LORD.'
(h) 'O Lord have mercy upon us.'
(i) 'Be imitators of me, as I am of Christ.'
(j) 'God exists.'
(k) 'I take you to be my husband.'
(l) 'I accept that Jesus was crucified.'
(m) 'I deplore the anti-Semitism of the mediaeval Church.'
(n) 'O come, O come Emmanuel! Redeem thy captive Israel.'
(o) 'I turn to Christ.'
(p) 'Thank you, Lord, for this food.'

TABLE 3

Illocutions	**Examples of religious use (sentences that are mainly characterised by this particular kind of illocution)**
CONSTATIVES – make (or deny) a factual claim – characterise *statements, assertions, predictions* and *hypotheses* – have a cognitive (descriptive) meaning/function	
EXPRESSIVES – express what the speaker feels or thinks – characterise *expressions of attitude, feeling, belief* and *intention* – have a non-cognitive meaning/function	(a) ['Holy, holy, holy Lord, God of power and might, heaven and earth are full of your glory.']

COMMISSIVES
- commit the speaker to an action or way of living, or accept an obligation
- characterise *agreements, commitments, promises* and *covenants*
- have a non-cognitive meaning/function

PRESCRIPTIVES
- lay some sort of obligation on the hearer
- characterise *commands, requests, questions* and *supplications*
- have a non-cognitive meaning/function

There is room for discussion and disagreement here, but I would classify (b), (j) and (l) as examples of religious language that are characterised by (or characteristically 'contain') *constatives*; (a), (m), (n) and (p) as characterised by *expressives*; (e), (g), (k) and (o) as characterised by *commissives*; and (c), (d), (f), (h) and (i) as characterised by *prescriptives*. (There is 'room for discussion' because speech acts may contain or carry more than one illocution; thus (e) carries expressive as well as commissive force, and (f) and (h) carry expressive as well as prescriptive force.)

Attitudes and beliefs

In the above exercise, 'God exists' (item (j)) raises a very important issue. I classified it as an example of a speech act characterised by a constative function, and you probably did the same. But we have noticed (pp. 71–73 and 85–86) that some radical theologians have interpreted this sentence very differently, arguing that 'God exists' does not state a fact about the existence of a creator or redeemer, or about any 'reality', but is to be understood in a non-realist sense as doing no more than expressing our commitment to a set of moral and spiritual values, and to a way of life based on them, for which the image of God is an appropriate symbol.

Approaching this debate from the other way round, it is usually claimed that expressions of religious attitudes, values, commitments and intentions *imply* claims about the real existence of God. We cannot, Brümmer argues, express our own trust in, or thanksgiving to, God 'without presupposing that this God exists in fact' (Brümmer, 1981, p. 268). In speech act terms, performing an illocution (whether expressive, commissive or prescriptive) *implies* 'the assertion of a constative in which the relevant facts are stated' (p. 29). Hence we cannot thank, praise, commit ourselves to or make requests of God without implying, in a way that *we* cannot deny, that this God exists.

Now it is certainly true that most religious believers and Christian theologians would say that, in the normal sense of these words, 'I believe in God' (that is, I recognise God as admirable, I am 'for' God and trust God) commits us to the implication that such a God really exists. Yet those who construe God in a non-realist fashion are not being inconsistent when they deny this, because for them God is only an *idea* or *ideal*. In the way that Cupitt and others understand expressions of religious attitudes, religious commitments and so on, these non-cognitive forms of religious language do *not* imply a cognitive claim about the real existence of God.

Those who have a conventional realist understanding of God should also acknowledge that some expressions of religious attitude do not imply belief in the manner described above. For example, expressing an attitude of universal, unqualified love (*agapé*) does not imply any claims about God's existence, and the same may be said for some other religious commitments and attitudes such as a willingness to forgive others, and some expressions of wonder or contemplation directed to the natural world. In a similar way, we might argue that people can be in favour of world peace, the universal acknowledgement of human rights or the ending of all human disease, and may even be said to put their 'trust' in such utopian states of affairs, without committing themselves to the belief that these situations have been 'realised' (and therefore now exist). As Archbishop William Temple once put it: 'I believe in one, holy, catholic and apostolic Church, but regret that it nowhere exists.' Many *ideals* do not exist in the sense of having instances in the real world; they only exist as *ideas*, 'in the mind'. If the word 'God' is understood symbolically as an ideal, therefore, the rules of implication that apply to trusting in realities such as people do not apply.

Moral speech acts

The speech act analysis can help us understand the multi-dimensional nature of morality (cf. Brümmer, 1981, p. 117). In making the moral judgement that a certain act or situation is 'good', the speaker is doing several things at once:

- *prescribing* the attitude other people should have to that act or situation;
- *expressing* the attitude he or she has to that act or situation, and by implication would have to all such acts or situations;
- *committing* himself or herself to a 'norm' or agreement of being for (or against) all such acts or situations;
- *implying* a range of constatives, particularly that of *asserting* that this act or situation is an example of this norm, but also (many would claim) that certain other facts are true – for example, facts about the existence of a value or of the will of God.

So we do quite a lot with our moral words! Let us try a particular example.

Example 3

If I say, 'Don't bully Susan', I perform a number of illocutionary acts.
- I express my attitude to ('what I feel about') your bullying of Susan (and other acts of bullying).
- I lay an obligation on you to adopt the same attitude to the bullying of Susan as I do.
- I commit myself to being against all similar acts of bullying ('Bullying is wrong').
- I imply that your act fell foul of this moral norm (hence *your* bullying *of Susan* was wrong) and – if I am a religious believer – that God disapproves of it.

Revisiting the speaking God

In Chapter 3 we looked at Nicholas Wolterstorff's defence of the claim that God may be said to 'speak' through Scripture. Speech act analysis is, in fact, central to his argument, for it distinguishes acts of uttering or inscribing (locutionary acts) from illocutionary acts of asking, asserting, commanding and promising that are performed by way of them, and focuses our attention on the latter. The possibility then arises that promises, commands, and so on, may be performed in other ways *and through other people and texts*, 'for one can tell somebody something by deputizing someone else to speak on one's behalf' (Wolterstorff, 1995, p. 13). Wolterstorff's claim that God speaks through others, especially through the writers of the biblical books, depends on this speech act analysis, with God being thought of as performing *illocutionary acts* of commanding, asserting, promising, etc., through the *locutions* of the prophets and other authors of Scripture. In the human world, acts such as signing, seconding or otherwise adopting a text enable the locution of another person to convey one's own illocutionary acts. Naturally, in the case of God the *manner* of appropriating or endorsing another's words is bound to be different; but the logic of the relationship appears to be more or less the same.

A famous example of this situation, cited by Wolterstorff, was the incident that precipitated St Augustine's conversion to Christianity. When he heard a child at play repeating the words, 'Take it and read', Augustine heard this as 'a divine command to open my book of Scripture and read the first passage on which my eyes should fall' (*Confessions*, VIII, section 12). The passage in question (Romans 13:13–14) was doubtless also interpreted by Augustine as God speaking to Augustine by way of what *Paul* had written.

Revisiting the language of worship

It is also useful to apply the speech act analysis to religious worship. As we saw above, worship contains specific examples of language by which illocutionary acts are performed, including prayerful requests, religious vows and expressions of trust, gratitude, longing and awe. But what about the *perlocutionary* function of the language of worship, that is, the actual *effects* of these linguistic acts? Most language is intended to have an effect – otherwise we would not bother to employ it; but we don't usually enquire what effects religious language has.

EXERCISE
What are the effects of the language of worship? Try to give as complete a list as you can, including not just intentional perlocutionary effects but also possible *unintentional* effects.

In situations of worship and prayer speech acts are primarily focused on God. Some – but by no means all – religious believers may think that God is affected by them, in the sense of being 'pleased' by the worshippers' promises and 'persuaded' by their pleas, or by responding with certain actions on God's own account (bestowing grace or revelation, entering a covenant with the worshippers, answering prayers, and so on). We might think of all this as the 'vertical' effects of worship. They are, of course, largely unknown to the worshipper, unless God reveals his 'pleasure' or gives a 'response' that we are forced to recognise as God's work.

But worship also has a more tangible and measurable 'horizontal' effect in human psychology and spirituality, as the speech acts of the worshipper evoke, sustain and deepen other people's religious and moral attitudes, beliefs and dispositions to certain forms of experience and behaviour. It also has a similar feedback or reinforcing effect onto the language user himself or herself. All of these may be described as the perlocutionary effects of worship and prayer. They are of signal importance in Christian nurture or formation. As the so-called 'faith community approach' to Christian education insists (Astley, 2000b, pp. 17–20), it is through the congregation's worship, particularly its celebration of Christ (perceived as the human face of God), that Christians are formed in the appropriate Christian attitudes, values and dispositions, and their related beliefs. Worshippers are thus conformed to the image of God in Christ. Worship therefore has a profoundly important *evocative* (perlocutionary), as well as an *expressive* (illocutionary) function (cf. Westerhoff, 1983; Astley, Francis and Crowder, 1996, section 7; Gill, 1999, pp. 218, 226).

But, of course, all this may sometimes go astray. The effect of worship on the worshippers Church themselves and others (and, presumably, on God) may be other than the Church intends or foresees. Much of the reform of the language of worship that has taken place since the 1960s has been driven by the sense that the older liturgies, hymns, prayers and Bible versions can disable worship, partly as a result of the effect they have on the worshippers. In the Anglican Church, for example, the language of the 1662 Prayer Book has been criticised (fairly or unfairly) for evoking too negative and untrustful an attitude to God by laying too much stress on the worshippers' sinfulness ('miserable offenders' who have 'erred and strayed like lost sheep' and in whom there is 'no health'), and for being too individualistic and not sufficiently full-blooded in its thanksgiving. By contrast, the language of modern liturgies is expected to promote more of a sense of real thanksgiving and confidence in God's forgiveness, and an atmosphere of *corporate* worship. Whether this is the case or not is clearly a question that cannot be decided without some empirical exploration of how people actually respond to different forms of religious language (cf. Astley, 1992).

EXERCISE

Compare and contrast some examples of present-day worship texts, alongside older versions of the same or similar forms of worship. Good examples might be individual prayers of confession, eucharistic prayers ('canons' or prayers of thanksgiving), whole services (such as baptism) or recent hymns and choruses (compare these with hymns from the nineteenth century in particular).

Do you think that the modern and the older examples of religious language are likely to differ in their effects on the attitudes, values, emotions and beliefs of the worshippers, and in what ways?

Further reading

Astley, J (1992), 'Christian worship and the hidden curriculum of Christian learning', in J Astley and D Day (eds), *The Contours of Christian Education*, chapter 10, Great Wakering, McCrimmons.

Astley, J; Francis, L J and Crowder, C (eds) (1996), *Theological Perspectives on Christian Formation: a reader*, Leominster, Gracewing, section 7.

Austin, J L (1962), *How to do Things with Words*, Oxford, Oxford University Press.

Brümmer, V (1981), *Theology and Philosophical Inquiry: an introduction*, London, Macmillan, chapter 2.

Caird, G B (1980), *The Language and Imagery of the Bible*, London, Duckworth, chapter 1.

Donovan, P (1976), *Religious Language*, London, Sheldon, chapter 7.

Jeffner, A (1972), *The Study of Religious Language*, London, SCM, chapters III and IV.

Smart, N (1972), *The Concept of Worship*, London, Macmillan, part one.

9. INTERPRETATION AND UNDERSTANDING

Introduction

When we talk it is usually in the expectation that someone is listening; and if we write (or email or text) we hope that someone will read what we have produced. The prime purpose of language is communication, and for that we need a recipient.

Often, however, that is where the trouble begins. I say (or write) this and that, but will you hear (understand) the message that I intend to communicate, or something different? And does it matter?

Reflecting on experience
Reflect on your experience as a listener to other people's conversations, talks, lectures or sermons, and as a reader of other people's books, newspapers, letters, poems, emails and text messages.

How important is it for you to understand what is in the speaker's mind? Are there situations in which that does not matter very much, or even at all?

Author-text-reader

It is a surprise to many people to learn that a substantial number of literary critics, and even biblical critics, claim that knowing the intentions of a speaker or writer is irrelevant to the task of understanding that we are engaged in as we listen to him speak, or (particularly) read her writings. We shall return to this claim later. But if the *author* isn't the key to all this, what is?

The view that the most important element is the *text* might seem to most people to concentrate too much on the 'inert wire' of a circuit, whereas this medium – like a text – has 'no life of its own'.

> It 'lives' only as an electric wire is alive. Its power originates elsewhere: in a human author. There is another point of comparison: however powerful the author's act of creation, the text lies impotent until it also comes into contact with a human reader. Only then can the human power, imagination, and intellect carried by the marks on a page strike a light, communicate warmth, or give a nasty shock. (Morgan with Barton, 1988, p. 269)

Readers are therefore important in their own right. Robert Morgan argues that the text has no rights, and while 'speakers and writers have some short-term right to be understood as they intended, . . . that right dies with them' (p. 270). In reading a text from the past, therefore, it is 'the interests or aims of the interpreters that are decisive, not the claims of the text as such' (p. 7).

On this analysis the reader-interpreter is more active, and more significant, than one might at first think. According to the great exponents of *hermeneutics*, the theory of interpretation, we are interpretative beings – for ever interpreting other voices, texts and situations. The interpreter (Latin, *inter*, between) is an in-between-person who explains or translates between one (person or text) and another.

The scholars of the Romantic Movement such as Schleiermacher were concerned that a reader should come to know the true meaning of a text by recovering, through empathetic imagination, its author's intended meaning. As readers, our task was to re-experience the author's original experience, putting ourselves 'in his shoes'; indeed, we should seek to understand the author better than he understood himself. But the view that the reader's main responsibility is to uncover the 'authorial intention' concealed behind the text has been vigorously challenged by scholars in the last century who insisted that writing distanced the author from his text and that, in any case, the interpreter had her own, highly significant, part to play.

Interpretation in process

Such a perspective has been coupled with the insight (drawn from Martin Heidegger and others) that, as interpreters, we always begin with a view or framework, and never as 'blank slates' or 'innocent eyes'. We bring our pre-understanding to all our encounters, always prejudging what a text or a thing or a person *means*. Indeed, according to Hans-Georg Gadamer, we can only understand at all *through* the employment of our 'legitimate prejudices' or pre-understandings.

> To try to escape from one's own concepts in interpretation is not only impossible but manifestly absurd. To interpret means precisely to bring one's own preconceptions into play so that the text's meaning can really be made to speak for us. (Gadamer, 1993, p. 358)

This relationship of interpreter to text is modelled on a *conversation* between two people. Understanding does not derive from the interpreter's monologue; it begins 'when something addresses us'. It is in this interaction between the reader and the other, which Gadamer expressed in the image of a *fusion of horizons*, that a new interpretation is forged that goes beyond them both. The metaphor of the 'horizon' stands for a 'range of vision' that includes the world-view or cultural assumptions of a particular standpoint. The two 'horizons' in question are those of the reader and the somewhat alien horizon of the text. Their fusion does not imply a swamping of the text's horizon by that of the reader, or vice-versa. Rather, 'the point is that the original meaning is accessible in no other way than through a fusion of horizons' (Stiver, 2001, p. 46). We can only understand the horizon of the other *through* our own.

While it is my interests, concerns and world-view that first open up and interrogate the text, it is the text that then questions and revises my understanding. This process is truly interactive:

> To reach an understanding in a dialogue is not merely a matter of putting oneself forward and successfully asserting one's own point of view, but being transformed into a communion in which we do not remain what we were. (Gadamer, 1993, p. 379)

The true dialogue of interpretation is therefore a thoroughly risky, because transformative, activity; the hermeneutical conversation demands that we put our own horizon at risk.

But in this 'genuine dialogue' change is not just on the side of the reader-interpreter, for 'something emerges that is contained in neither of the partners by himself'; in assimilating the text, there is 'a new creation of understanding' (Gadamer, 1993, pp. 462, 473). Interpretative understanding is therefore 'not merely a reproductive but always a productive activity as well' (Gadamer, 1993, p. 296); hence understanding is never passive, but an active, constructive activity.

EXERCISE

How do you respond to these analogies of (a) a 'conversation' between the reader and the text, and (b) a 'fusion of their horizons' that results in a new understanding that is contained in neither partner by itself?

How might these ideas be applied to biblical texts?

The metaphorical conversation or dialogue (or 'dialectic') in which I am engaged as a reader gives rise to an interpretation that may well be different from the view taken by other readers or hearers whose context is different. Any text is therefore open to a great variety of new interpretations. While some writers in this field embrace a radical relativism of readings, with no one reading being privileged over the rest, others argue that some interpretations may be said to be better than others, for in them the 'right questions' are asked of the text and the listener is able to hear the 'right answers'. If this is the case, the text cannot just mean anything we want it to mean.

Whose tradition is it anyway?

The stress on the importance of our prejudgements is often taken to imply that we do not and cannot stand outside history. Gadamer argued that we always stand within a tradition and that there is no way of freeing ourselves from it: 'history does not belong to us; we belong to it' (1993, p. 276). We are already linked to the texts of the past, and it is our link to the past that enables us to understand the past. Our present horizon is itself the result of many of these fusions of present and past horizons, with the tradition giving us the presuppositions that enable us to understand and question it. In this way, it is history and tradition that prepare us to understand the past and its texts.

But the link also runs backwards. Instead of sharply and rigidly distinguishing between what a text 'meant' then and what it 'means' now, Gadamer argues that we should think of each influencing the other, in both directions. Thus our sense of what a text means when it is applied in our present context will influence, at least implicitly, what we think the text meant in the past (Gadamer, 1993, p. 308).

Moving in circles?

The claim that interpretation moves in circles is a common feature of discussion in hermeneutics, and appears first in Schleiermacher. The *hermeneutical circle* has come to be used to describe several processes (hermeneutical *spiral* would be better, for although we re-turn again and again to the text, each visit is at a different level of understanding). They include the following:

- the way the interpreter must relate the parts of a work to the whole, and the whole to its parts:

  > understanding a whole stretch of language or literature depends on an understanding of its component parts, while an understanding of these smaller units depends, in turn, on an understanding of the total import of the whole. (Thiselton, 1980, p. 104)

- the way that the interpreter's own framework, presuppositions or viewpoint, which are what enables her to question and interpret the text, are reshaped by the text itself (and so on and on): 'any interpretation which is to contribute understanding, must already have understood what is to be interpreted' (Heidegger, 1962, p. 194);
- the way that (for example, in biblical interpretation) we may begin with a naïve fascination for the text which 'speaks so directly to us', and then adopt a critical stance towards it, interrogating it suspiciously, before returning to a *second naïveté* in which it regains its power to communicate (see p. 108 below).

Conservation or criticism?

Jürgen Habermas, of the 'Frankfurt School' of Critical Theory, argued that Gadamer's account did not leave enough room for a criticism of the tradition, or of our pre-understandings and the way they have been shaped by tradition. Habermas contends that we must be able to question tradition and engage in a moral, and therefore political, criticism of the deception that language often practises in legitimating ideologies. The approach of people like Gadamer, by contrast, is inherently conservative.

EXERCISE

In reading a text, particularly a scriptural text, how important is it to inject an element of criticism?

Gadamer responded that there is always a critical interaction between our present horizon and the horizon of the past; he assumes 'the possibility of our taking a critical stance with regard to every convention' (Gadamer, 1993, p. 547). Our world-view is not swamped or absorbed by the past; we always have the right to challenge and check the claims of any text. However,

- even this process is in the end hermeneutical;
- criticism is itself a tradition; and
- we can never escape the fact that it is *we*, the inheritors of a tradition, who are the ones who engage in the criticism.

Other writers have sought to find more room for a critical element in the process of interpretation. Thus Paul Ricoeur distinguishes between a *hermeneutics of recollection*, which helps us retrieve the message of a past text for our own age, and a *hermeneutics of suspicion* that questions the distorting effect of ideology, especially that which results from unconscious motivations within its message. This second element is what allows us to reform and revise the linguistic tradition that we inherit.

Ricoeur argued that in reading texts we need to adopt a (paradoxical) combination of criticism and conservation.

> Hermeneutics seems to me to be animated by this double motivation: willingness to suspect, willingness to listen; vow of rigor, vow of obedience. In our time we have not finished doing away with *idols* and we have barely begun to listen to *symbols*. (Ricoeur, 1970, p. 27)

That is to say, after they have been purged by the critical fires, including in our case those of biblical criticism, we must return to our texts. Our analysis of Scripture must move on to a post-critical understanding ('appropriation' or 'application'), the stage of a *second naïveté* 'in and through criticism'. Notice that Ricoeur does not see criticism as a destructive power which puts a stop to our inheriting the tradition and its wisdom. He acknowledges that 'beyond the desert of criticism, we wish to be called again', and he holds out the hope that 'it is by *interpreting* that we can *hear* again' (Ricoeur, 1969, pp. 349, 351). It is this that encourages us to press on. 'If the other side is already in view, however dimly, one may venture more willingly into the desert' (Stiver, 2001, p. 139).

Dan Stiver notes that this dialectic of affirmation and critique is not foreign to Scripture and Christian tradition, but is an integral part of them (Stiver, 2001, pp. 157–159). In the Old Testament, for example, the theology ('ideology') of Israel's election was subject to the devastating criticism of the prophetic denunciation of her apostasy and injustice. So the sacred texts that Christians and others interpret are already imbued with a self-critical spirit.

While Ricoeur, like Gadamer, argues that we need to allow for – and indeed embrace – the idea that there will be many interpretations of a text, he agrees that this does not mean that a text can mean just anything. David Tracy's notion of a *classic text* may be relevant at this point. This is a text that is viewed as having an earned authority in the tradition. Such a text exerts a 'claim to attention, a vexing, a provocation'. We are always at risk in attempting to interpret religious classics, the risk being that of 'entering the most dangerous conversation of all' by 'being caught up in, even being played by, the questions and answers' (Tracy, 1981, pp. 154–155). (Gadamer makes a similar point about being seized by meaning by any text, as opposed to dominating the action ourselves.)

EXERCISE

The image here is of a conversation between two very unequal partners, in which one is said *rightly* to dominate.

Is this a helpful analysis of the Christian reader's relationship with the Bible?

Holey discourse?

We should never underestimate the other partner in the hermeneutical conversation – the ever-present, ever-active interpreter. *Reader-response theory* is an influential perspective in biblical studies which develops this emphasis that meaning occurs in the interaction between text and reader, and requires both. Wolfgang Iser introduced the notion of 'blanks' or 'gaps' within the narrative of a text, arguing that the silences are as important as what is said. These gaps draw the reader in, and the reader then fills them in or fleshes them out, 'filling the blanks with projections'. '[The reader] is drawn into the events and made to supply what is meant from what is not said. . . . But as the unsaid comes to life in the reader's imagination, so the said "expands" to take on greater significance' (Iser, 1980, p. 111). No text can say everything, not if it is to engage the reader. Hence:

> the work exists only as it is read, when the reader composes the meaning based on the structure and guidance supplied by the text. The structure of the text therefore guides but does not fully determine the reader's response. (Stiver, 1996, p. 109)

EXERCISE

Reflect on the gaps in the story of Jesus, such as the application of much of his teaching (e.g. the parables) or the historical context of an event (what happened before this, what happened afterwards, what was Judas doing when it was taking place?). You might want to think about other types of gaps: for example, Jesus' physical appearance or marital status, his sense of humour, tone of voice or the way he looked at people.

Does your imagination fill these gaps in a particular way? How does this affect your reading of the recorded story of Jesus?

Away from the controversial area of the biblical text, the idea of filling gaps sounds even more plausible. One common example of religious discourse is the *sermon*. When churchgoers listen to sermons there is an implicit, hermeneutical conversation taking place in which the listener in the pew discovers meaning *between* the preacher and herself.

Part of what is going on is that the listeners are preaching their own sermons to themselves in the metaphorical spaces and silences they have found within the preacher's sermon. As Sam Keen has argued, with regard to a related form of communication:

> the lectures I thought were best, the most logically finished and closed, gave no way to the student to get involved in them. The ones with interstices drew them in, and they became colleagues with me in a wrestling with the mysteries. (Fowler and Keen, 1978, p. 158)

One could argue that when a sermon, with its images, stories and arguments, catalyses those who hear it so that they preach their own sermons to themselves, it conforms to the Gospel principle of the leavening of the dough (Matthew 13:33), for the growth that it creates in the listener is neither extra yeast nor additional dough, but a 'new creation'. The effective sermon listener is very active – but silently so – as she probes, questions, reflects and launches off in a new direction: making the preacher's thoughts her own by creating her own thoughts in response. In these ways, it may be argued, the word of God is re-preached, re-heard and renewed in its hearers.

Text appeal

I have passed over the nature of the text itself in a rather cavalier fashion. It should be pointed out that in the second half of the twentieth century a new interest in the text also arose within literary criticism. *Structuralism* investigated the text through the patterns (elements in relation) that it was thought to exemplify: its 'deep structures' which reflected the structure of the minds (including the author's mind) that imposed meaning on the world. The focus here is on the text and the world of the text, rather than on the reader or on reconstructing the historical process behind the text.

In its turn structuralism largely fell prey to the ravages of *post-structuralism*, a species of post-modernism that seeks to *deconstruct* the text. The key figure here is the controversial Jacques Derrida, who criticised structuralism's tendency to privilege speech over writing and presence over absence. For Derrida, 'to write is to draw back':

> *To leave* writing is to be there only in order to provide its passageway, to be the diaphanous elements of its going forth . . . For the work, the writer is at once everything and nothing. Like God. (Derrida, 1978, p. 70)

On Derrida's account meaning does not exist except in and through language, or 'meaningful signification': 'there is nothing [that is, nothing expressible] outside of the text' (1976, p. 158). Nevertheless, the text itself is to be deconstructed in order to show its inevitable ambiguity and lack of clarity, phenomena that result in a play of interpretation to which there is no end and therefore no limit. *Difference* determines meaning, for the meaning of a term depends on its difference from other terms and is never fully present in the term by itself. Therefore meaning is never fixed; it is always 'deferred' and therefore elusive.

It might appear from all this that relativism and nihilism have conquered all. There are, it would seem, no thoughts and no facts prior to the language of someone's signification – that is, prior to someone's asserting that something is the case. Author and reader exist in this perspective, but only just; *the text is all*. But Derrida (who is a *very* difficult writer) has denied this view of his work, arguing that deconstruction is actually an openness towards the other, which incorporates a recognition of the limitation of all such language to describe the other and a recognition of the alienating and exploitative uses of all language.

Author's rights?

I have already indicated that many critics routinely ignore the intentions of a text's author. 'The birth of the reader,' it is said, 'must be at the cost of the death of the Author' (Barthes, 1977, p. 148). But is this position justified? Paul Ricoeur is another scholar who has pointed out the radical difference between a real dialogue that involves face-to-face contact with the speaker and the 'dialogue' of a reader faced by a 'distanciated text', which is really a 'conversation' that takes place in the absence of the author. In this latter case:

- (normally) the author is wholly inaccessible and his text is not addressed to us anyway; there is therefore no communication between the act of writing and the act of reading, and 'the writer does not respond to the reader' (Ricoeur, 1981, pp. 146–147);
- the text is distanced from its originating situation (contrast a real dialogue in which words such as 'I', 'you' and 'it' refer to something in the immediate situation, to which the speaker can point);
- 'the text's career escapes the finite horizon lived by its author. What the text says now matters more than what the author meant to say' (p. 201).

As the text takes on a life of its own, what is important is the world 'in front of the text', a world that the reader can inhabit, not the world that lies 'behind' it.

Ricoeur (along with many others) seems to argue that, in a situation like this, uncovering the author's intention is not really an option. And, in any case, everything of value has already been lodged in the text. But is this last point true?

> **EXERCISE**
> What do you think? Is it plausible to argue that everything that we need to interpret a text already lies within the text, and that the intentions of the author are both inaccessible and irrelevant?

This thesis works well with poetry, but it is less plausible with history or biography, or if we are faced by a story that we cannot tell whether to treat as fact or fiction. Some argue that, in order to discover what such texts are about, we have to 'exit the sense of the text and uncover the relevant non-linguistic features of the context of the discourse'. In particular, we have to use our knowledge about what the writer probably intended to say, so as to discover what was 'the content and stance of the authorial discourse' (Wolterstorff, 1995, pp. 150, 153; cf. p. 200). As Wolterstorff convincingly argues:

> We sometimes respond to what we regard as far-fetched interpretations with the exclamation, 'I can't imagine how anyone could possibly have meant that with those words!' Thereby we give voice to our recognition of the outer boundaries. If we can't imagine someone saying that with those words, then we won't accept that as an interpretation of them. (p. 177)

On this account, interpreters cannot operate without a set of beliefs about the text's author, which allows them to judge the relative probability of the author having intended to say one thing rather than another. Although Wolterstorff does *not* see this as trying to get into the mind of the author, the main difficulty with his account is that (as Ricoeur and others insist) we may be too distant from our authors, and know too little about them, to be very confident of our judgements in such matters.

Further reading

Jeanrond, W G (1994), *Theological Hermeneutics: development and significance*, London, SCM.

Pailin, D A (1986), *Groundwork of Philosophy of Religion*, London, Epworth, chapter 4.

Pattison, G (2001), *A Short Course in the Philosophy of Religion*, London, SCM, chapter 6.

Schökel, L A (1998), *A Manual of Hermeneutics*, ET Sheffield, Sheffield Academic Press.

Stiver, D R (1996), *The Philosophy of Religious Language: sign, symbol and story*, Oxford, Blackwell, chapters 5 and 8.

Thiselton, A C (1992), *New Horizons in Hermeneutics*, London, HarperCollins, chapters IX, X, XI and XIV.

Wolterstorff, N (1995), *Divine Discourse: philosophical reflections on the claim that God speaks*, Cambridge, Cambridge University Press, chapter 13.

10. THE PRACTICAL THEOLOGY AND ETHICS OF GOD-TALK

Introduction

In the context of a discussion of moral decision-making and 'the role of cultural specificities' in Christian practice, Rowan Williams comments that 'Christians learn their faith in incarnate ways.' He adds that no one learns their Christianity 'without a local accent'; all 'speak of God with a marked local accent' (Williams, 2001, pp. 8–9). I intend to steal this image.

Regional accents are more acceptable in Britain than they once were. Short 'a's, no longer limited to local radio, are now common on Radio 4; and television programmes such as Coronation Street, Eastenders and Brookside have hired actors who would never have had anything more than silent walk-on parts in the 1950s. Even the farming dynasties in the Archers sound less posh than they did. In the churches things are changing too, and there is much more of a chance that the local vicar will sound as truly local as the Methodist minister and Catholic priest routinely did.

But accent is a touchy thing. It is hard not to be suspicious of someone who speaks in a way that is different from our own, and sometimes demeaned by them. I still smart from an occasion nearly forty years ago when the manager of a bookshop in my university town took pains to correct my pronunciation of my own name . . .

All this talk of accents is, of course, a figure of speech. Our God-talk also comes in 'accents'. Those who learn to speak of and to God show the marks of the context of that learning. Here 'local accent' (and 'local dialect') stands for the content, form and style of religious discourse that reflects their age, gender, class, upbringing, form of education, spirituality, and so on (and on). It is all likely to be very personal.

Criticising and correcting another's speech is part and parcel of education, and indeed of Christian formation (for there are right and wrong ways of speaking of God). It is unavoidable. But there is a pastoral responsibility here that cannot be ignored, even in the interests of the greater clarity, coherence and orthodoxy of our religious language. Those who speak of God need to treat one another's accents gently.

Reflecting on experience

How do you feel about your own God-talking? Are you keen to defend your way of speaking of God in discussion with others, or do you prefer to keep quiet? And do you think that these two options only represent differences in personality, or are we naturally protective of our local religious accents?

In this chapter I shall try to address a number of pastoral and practical issues that relate to the use of religious language. Throughout the discussion, it may be helpful to keep in mind not only this metaphor of local accents, but also the different emphases of those who celebrate diversity of speech, *and* of those who seek to iron out differences and silence the overtones of context, so that we all end up sounding exactly the same.

Telling our stories in God

In Chapter 4 we touched on the importance of story as the way in which we all frame our human identity, telling ourselves and others who we really are, and as the way in which some speak of the divine and of God's relationship with the human world. In this section I want to integrate these themes.

> Who am I? The answer is a story, an intricate tale of action and insight, details and emerging order; a tale for the Christian not just of the self, but of the self in the hands of the living God. (TeSelle, 1975, p. 176)

EXERCISE
How do you respond to this claim?

How do you talk about yourself to people who really care about who you are?

Reflect on how others (particularly children) introduce themselves at the beginning of a friendship. Would you describe this as 'telling a story'?

James Fowler has researched the development of human faith, which he takes to be a central feature of all human life, identifying up to six stages. (Some now think of these as faith *styles*, rejecting the notion of development.) According to Fowler, faith is to be understood as 'the composing or interpreting of an ultimate environment [that is, what we take to be ultimate] *and* as a way-of-being-in relation to it' (Fowler and Keen, 1978, p. 25). Religious faith differs from other examples of faith only in having specific and explicit religious objects or contents. But all faith has content, identified by Fowler as that in which we believe and trust, which we recognise as ultimate, and to which we give our hearts. We all believe in *something*. Faith's content comprises the 'centres of value', 'images of power' and 'master stories' by which we live our lives (Fowler, 1981, pp. 276–277).

Fowler tells an anecdote of a chance companion in a taxi who told him, 'If we have any purpose on this earth, it is just to keep things going. We can stir the pot while we are here and try to keep things interesting. Beyond that everything runs down: your marriage runs down, your body runs down, your faith runs down. We can only try to make it interesting' (Fowler and Keen, 1978, p. 23; cf. Fowler, 1981, pp. 277–279). 'Stirring the pot' because 'everything runs down' is this man's *master story*; it is the dominating story-metaphor by which he lived, the myth of his life.

According to Cupitt, stories are theological in four ways.

> Every story just by being a story constitutes a promise that life can be meaningful. That is the job of stories; they make life make sense. Secondly, every story has, is and conveys a moral in the sense of a piece of practical wisdom about life. The man in the tavern who tells you his

story is telling you what life has taught him. We all have at least one message that we want to give to our fellow humans – our own story. Thirdly, every story inculcates values: it is strongly action-guiding or regulative. Stories teach people by what values they should live. Finally, stories in the telling define the identities of their own leading characters. (Cupitt, 1991, p. 77)

EXERCISE

What would you identify as the master story, myth or narrative by which you live *your* life?

If there is more than one, do they conflict?

Human beings are inveterate storytellers. Story-telling is natural to us, for the story's duration – its continuing over and through time – matches the nature of our experience, which is also essentially narrative in form. Further, as John Drane has remarked, 'it is not possible to read or hear a story without it impinging on our own story, or even becoming our story' (Drane, 2000, p. 140).

According to Paul Ricoeur, the important thing for readers of a text is that they should immerse themselves in the world that is expressed in it, and then apply this to their own lives so as to understand themselves better. Thomas Groome argues that our Christian education only really takes off when a dialogue or conversation is joined between our 'story' (and our related 'vision') on the one hand, and the Christian story and vision – or, better, stories and visions – on the other (Groome, 1980, chapters 9 and 10; 1991, part II). (By the expression 'our story and vision', Groome means our experience of our own engagement in the world, our expression of ourselves and our hope for the future.) What happens in this interchange is that the stories and promises of the tradition confront our own biographies and hopes. The 'Christian story' then affirms parts of our own stories, but also challenges other parts before it pushes us towards action that is more faithful to itself. But our own stories also take some initiative, affirming much of the past story but condemning some of it (such as Christianity's condoning of slavery), and moving us beyond any simple repetition or imitation of the story as it has been handed down to us. Such an analysis offers a close educational parallel to Gadamer's account of a fusion of horizons in the act of interpretation (see above pp. 105–106).

Telling God's story slant

One major function of religious language is communicating religious truth, particularly in evangelism (preaching the Christian Gospel) and apologetics (arguing in favour of Christianity). It is natural to portray this communication as best achieved by means of a very clear, explicit and direct form of communication. But some have argued, at least in the case of evangelism, that religious teaching is at its most effective when it is done *indirectly*.

Søren Kierkegaard was a champion of what he called *indirect communication*. In this process, which is quite opposite to didactic teaching (that is, instruction or authoritarian teaching), the other person is engaged not by the directness and clarity of our message, but through its ambiguity and even its contradictions. The communicator approaches people and awakens their subjectivity 'from behind', as it were, 'manoeuvring them into a position from which they themselves, as a result of interior reflection, could step back and make a radical choice between remaining where they were and opting for a fundamental change' (Gardiner, 1988, p. 38; Pattison, 1997, pp. 4–5, 27–28, 89). Kierkegaard's own account of the process uses the powerful image of saying something 'to a passer-by in passing', without stopping him to discuss it and 'without attempting to persuade him to go the same way, but giving him instead an impulse to go precisely his own way' (Kierkegaard, 1941, p. 247).

According to Kierkegaard, this is the only way to ensure an authentic response to the authentic Gospel message. It is through the very indirection of this mode of sideways communication that the message has its effect, without laying itself open to objectification or taming. 'The intention of the teacher is to manifest content in such a way that the content escapes attempts to make it fixed, secured, ordered, understood, and tolerable. At the same time, this content *seduces* into rapt attention' (Harris, 1991, p. 70).

An influential paper by John Tinsley illuminates this process. It takes its title from the first line of Emily Dickinson's poem:

Tell all the Truth but tell it slant –
Success in Circuit lies
Too bright for our infirm Delight
The Truth's superb surprise

As Lightning to the Children eased
With explanation kind
The Truth must dazzle gradually
Or every man be blind –
(Dickinson, 1970, pp. 506–507)

Tinsley argues that the proper communication of the Gospel must be just such a self-effacing and indirect communication, for 'the gospel is not only *what* is said, but *how* it is said':

'Telling it slant' is more than an appropriate form of the gospel; it is its essential content, a manner incumbent upon the Christian communicator by the very nature of the gospel. (Tinsley, 1996, p. 88, cf. p. 92)

Jesus is a 'prophet of indirect communication': he is indirect about himself ('Let me ask you a question') and about the Kingdom of God ('It does not come with observation'). As we have seen in Chapter 4, the Jesus of the Synoptic gospels describes the nature and intentions of God in parables, many of which are deeply paradoxical and ambiguous, even ironic. Tinsley argues that Jesus presents us with a God of hiddenness who is spoken of in a provisional, incomplete revelation (p. 93).

The theme of indirection is also taken up by Kenneth Cragg in his discussion of the informal, *human* medium of biblical revelation. Cragg distinguishes this chancy process from the model of infallible revelation in Islam, in which the 'text does not in any way participate in the texture of its reception' (Cragg, 1981, p. 24). He argues that the New Testament literature could not have come about on this Islamic principle of verbal, direct revelation; it is, rather, indirect and incarnational. The way we treat the words of these sacred scriptures must be appropriate to the 'hazardous' form, context and mechanics of Jesus' own teaching ministry, as well as to the manner of their mediation, reception and dissemination. As Cragg insists, 'One cannot well infallibilize what does not come that way' (p. 25). In a powerful image he writes:

The Sermon on the Mount, assuming we have it, is first lost upon the winds of Galilee to be housed within the reverent recollection of that

bunch of men and women who were all that Jesus left when, undocu-
mented and undocumenting, he went into his Gethsemane. (Cragg,
1981, p. 25)

EXERCISE

How convincing do you find this account of indirect communication? What are its advantages and disadvantages?

Can you think of good examples of indirect Christian communication in Scripture or the Church's liturgies and
hymns?

One element of 'indirection' that is often overlooked is the widespread
analogical and (particularly) metaphorical forms of religious language,
including parables and myths (see Chapters 4 and 5 above). The allusive,
suggestive and imprecise language of metaphors generates 'slantwise' or
'lateral' ways of thinking about God, not least because metaphorical
statements 'always contain the whisper, "it is *and it is not*"' (McFague,
1983, p. 13).

Sex and sanctity

In Chapter 1 we glanced at Ursula Le Guin's distinction between two
forms of discourse: the 'mother tongue' and 'the father tongue'. For Le
Guin, this is largely a gender distinction.

EXERCISE

How convincing is this distinction between (a) the language
of conversation, which Le Guin says 'we learn . . . from our
mothers and speak . . . to our kids', but which many men
'learn not to speak at all'; and (b) the language of one-way
communication and objectivity, of social power and success,
which she designates the 'father tongue' (Le Guin, 1989, pp.
147–151)?

It is arguable that many such distinctions between men and women may be better characterised, not as rigid markers of differences between the sexes, but rather as differences between 'masculine' and 'feminine' outlooks, attitudes, orientations or viewpoints. (Stereotypically 'masculine' characteristics may be dominant in some women, just as stereotypically 'feminine' characteristics are in some men.) Notwithstanding this caveat, Le Guin's gendered account of language may be illuminating alongside the more rigorous work of 'sociolinguists' on the differences between how men and women use language.

According to Deborah Tannen, women don't speak or ask questions just to get information, as men tend to do. This is nicely illustrated by the story of the couple driving down a motorway, when the woman asks, 'Do you want to stop for a coffee at the next service-station?' The man immediately replies, 'No' – because he doesn't. But he has misunderstood the message. The question in the car was an 'invitation to intimacy', an opening move in what was meant to be a *conversation*; it was part of what Tannen calls 'rapport-talk'. The man responded as if he were still at work, and had been asked if he needed a number 6 masonry bit or whether he knew the price of pig-iron in Tokyo. Women do not (usually) speak just to convey neutral facts across intervening spaces ('report-talk'); men (often) do.

> For most women, the language of conversation is primarily a language of rapport: a way of establishing connections and negotiating relationships . . . For most men, talk is primarily a means to preserve independence and negotiate and maintain status in a hierarchical social order. (Tannen, 1992, p. 77)

Women speak in order to talk, then, and talk in order to share a relationship. When they complain that men don't understand them, it is partly because men don't understand *that*.

EXERCISE

Does this chime in with your own experience?

If Tannen is correct in her analysis, what implications does it have for *religious* language?

From my experience of research interviews with women and men, and from more anecdotal evidence, I should like to suggest that this difference between men and women carries over into their religious language. I have claimed elsewhere that the language of women (or of the more 'feminine' personality) is in its own way *disinterested* talk, but in a fashion that is wholly different from the disinterested objectivity of academic-speak or Le Guin's 'father tongue'.

> Women's talk in general is not a distancing discourse, apt for competitive disagreements; rather it is disinterested in the sense that it is without a purpose ulterior to the expression and maintenance of a relationship. I wonder if this is why women's talk *about* God often sounds so close, in the content and manner of their speech, to talking *to* God; whereas on the whole men tend to distinguish these two modes of religious language. (Astley, 2002, p. 79)

Religious self-expression, particularly in prayer and worship, does appear to be largely a matter of mother-tongue work, in the sense that it too is primarily concerned with 'keeping the relationship going' and expressing how one feels about things (another's suffering, or one's own disappointments and joys), and not about getting things done or securing some advantage. Bryan Spinks writes that all prayer is 'the language of lovers' (Spinks, 1991, p. 99). Such discourse is truly 'without any ulterior interest'; it serves no end beyond the relationship and the needs of the other. In the best examples there is no thought of any reward, except of doing God's will. Pastoral God-talk shares some of the same qualities. When visiting the bereaved, 'some things require saying and originality is not what's looked for' (Williams, 2000b, p. 75). Nor are prayer and pastoral care about power, but love and relationships; they are forms of talk that involve no arguments and identify no winners and losers. In these contexts the speaker should feel no lust for conclusions or cleverness. If it is the case that these are particularly feminine forms of God-talk, we should not be surprised to find them more frequently illustrated by females. (There has to be *some* explanation for the fact that there are far more women in church congregations than there are men.)

By contrast, my sense is that 'men tend to be more distanced in their God-talk: more analytic, speculative, "cool" and detached.' They are perhaps more at ease in talking *about* God, therefore, because they are more ready in this mode to debate, to argue, and to clarify and defend a position. 'Many of them seem to find conceptual analysis and sparring over intellectual positions more in keeping with their natural way of speaking, and perhaps of living' (Astley, 2002, p. 80).

Nicola Slee's research on women's faith development is worth quoting here. It is based on a careful analysis of in-depth interviews with female interviewees, all of them graduates. Her study throws up some themes in her respondents' 'faithing strategies' that *may* be particularly characteristic of women:

> First, there is a dominance of concrete, visual, narrative and embodied forms of thinking over propositional, abstract or analytical thought. Whilst conceptual thought was not absent from the interviews, there was a marked preference amongst the majority of the women for a more concrete language of metaphor, story or exemplar as the vehicle for the expression of their faith experience. . . . Second, there is a dominance of personalised and relational forms of appropriating faith over abstract and impersonal means: faith was worked out in relation to the other, and this is demonstrated in the preference for metaphors emerging from personal life and relationship, the use of exemplars drawn from personal life and narratives centred around issues of inclusion and exclusion from communities of belonging, as well as in the conversational nature of the interview itself, in which faith was articulated in dialogue with the presence of the other. Third, each of the faithing strategies is rooted in a dynamic context of meaning-making in which the *process* of the interaction between interviewer and interviewee is as significant as the content. It was not only *what* was said, but the *way* in which it was said . . . which indicated the nature and style of the women's faith. (Slee, 2004, pp. 79–80)

If it *is* true that the nature of religious discourse tends to differ in these ways between men and women, or at least between 'masculine' and 'feminine' personality types or approaches, this might explain why men's 'cooler' and more 'objective' God-talk sometimes seems closer to the conceptual theology of the academic style of speech, whereas women's religious language may seem more *religious* – in the sense that it tends to employ more concrete, metaphorical, narrative and personal ways of thinking. We might argue, then, that women's God-talk – on the whole, and over the average, of course with *many* exceptions – is more of a 'metaphorical' theology (McFague/TeSelle) or 'mother-tongue theology' (Le Guin). As such, it is rooted more strongly in the primary religious discourse of Bible and prayer than is the distancing father tongue preferred by men.

According to Sallie McFague (1983, pp. 8–10), *feminist theology* has focused on religious language for three main reasons.

- Women are excluded from the world of religion when they are not allowed, alongside the men, to 'name' that world. The adoption of 'inclusive language' is one way in which this situation may be remedied. Recent changes both in formal liturgical language and in informal usage are highly relevant here.
- Much Christian language is patriarchal in character. Most of the images of deity (king, father, husband, master) are masculine and need complementing by feminine models if our views of the God who transcends gender, and the ways we order our human relationships, is to escape this taint of patriarchy. McFague also recommends that we complement masculine and feminine imagery with a model that is not gender-specific, the model of God as *friend* (McFague, 1983, pp. 178–192).
- When female images are applied to God their human source is elevated in importance. 'One of the functions of religious language . . . is "naming ourselves" as we "name" God', hence 'images that are excluded are not legitimated and honored'.

Nicola Slee's book in the present series offers an excellent introduction to feminist theology. Chapter 3 is devoted to religious language, and she argues there that:

> The way in which we speak about God has a profound, if mysterious, impact upon our understanding of and attitudes towards our own humanity and that of our neighbours, and shapes behaviour in powerful and subtle ways. . . . When God is spoken of only in male terms . . . the implicit message to women is that masculinity is somehow more god-like, nearer to godliness, preferred in some way over against femininity, and that to be female is not to be capable of imaging the divine nature. (Slee, 2003, pp. 25–27)

EXERCISE

What do you think of Nicola Slee's claims outlined in the above passage?

Theological listening

In the first chapter I argued in defence of a notion of 'ordinary theology' which, like Farley's interpretation of the original meaning of the word theology, is not to be thought of as restricted to the scholar, the teacher or the clergy. This *lay* theology, defined as the reflective God-talk of those who have little or no (scholarly and academic) theological education, is very widespread indeed.

It is, however, routinely ignored. Although many definitions of the word theology begin democratically, understanding it in terms of a person's God-talk or reflective speaking of the divine, most of them go on to limit its arena of application to the most sophisticated and disciplined forms of reflection. In this way, apart from a polite nod in the direction of a more generic or broader interpretation of the term, theology becomes restricted to an activity for academics.

This can be a disastrous position to adopt, however, for more than one reason. In particular, those engaged in the ministries of Christian communication, pastoral care and worship must acknowledge that the people who receive their ministrations also have a theology. And the clergy need to know what it is. Pastors and preachers must become sufficiently familiar with the religious beliefs and thoughts of those for whom they care and to whom they preach, and their patterns and modes of religious thinking and believing.

They therefore need to *listen* to them. Listening is a deeply pastoral act, partly because it is a mark of respect. If ministers care what their congregations – and their non-churchgoing parishioners – think, they should want to listen to them. The best sorts of pastoral preachers take the effort to listen to their congregations, recognising that 'the preacher's ears and heart must be open to the members of the parish as they are open to the Lord' (Jabusch, 1980, p. 54). This listening should include an element of what might be called *theological listening* – listening out for theology. The justification for this claim is that people's often halting and inarticulate speech can and does constitute a form of theology. Such an ordinary theology may lack the systematic coherence of more literate forms, but it will often make up for this deficit by revealing a closer connection with the religious impulses and with their outworkings in secular living. In other words, it will be closer both to faith and to life. But ordinary theology – and, indeed, ordinary atheology (unbelief) – will only be heard by those with ears that are attuned to it.

EXERCISE

From what you know of particular Christian preachers, ministers and communicators, how would you rate them as 'theological listeners'?

What are the pastoral and theological implications of theological listening?

Listening out for theology is itself a theological act (Browning, 1991, p. 286). It is not always an easy one. To succeed at it priests, preachers and pastors will often need to listen to their 'flocks' more intently and in more depth than some of them presently do. This should at least prevent them from dismissing outright those examples of God-talk that appear on the surface to consist of nothing but banalities, self-contradictions and even superstitions, but which are in fact much more profound than this – and in any case may be undergirded by a deep faith. In listening for ordinary theology, ministers will have to burrow below this superficial level, so as to uncover the 'depth grammar' of a person's faith, which represents how they *really* speak of God and talk religion.

It is surely worth the trouble; not least because 'ordinary theologians' may just sometimes have got it right.

> We learn about God in the way a grammarian of language discovers the rules. He masters the language and assesses carefully what we all have access to already, our common working speech. So the theologian gets no new revelation and has no special organ for knowledge. He is debtor to what we, in one sense, have already – the Scriptures and the lives and thoughts of the faithful. . . . This puts theology within the grasp of conscientious tentmakers, tinkers like Bunyan, lay people like Brother Lawrence, and maybe someone you know down the street who shames you with his or her grasp. . . . Theology is often done by the unlikely. . . . God's ways are still discovered by his friends and not in virtue of techniques and agencies of power. (Holmer, 1978, p. 21)

On speaking personally

Of course, such ordinary God-talk is usually highly personal, and will often seem to the expert ill-framed and badly worded. But the word 'personal' is rarely used as a pejorative epithet, except when it is applied to someone else. And no Christian, not even a parson or a scholar, has the right to be snooty or high-brow about other people's faith. As D Z Phillips puts it, we need to find room for 'the ugly, the banal and the vulgar for these, too, may be forms of religious belief' (Phillips, 1993, p. 250). He recounts a telling incident:

> I recall an elderly widow asking me why God had called her two sons home before her. She proceeded to provide her own answer. She said that if she went into a garden to pick flowers, she would not choose weeds, but the best blooms. In taking her sons to himself, God had picked the best blooms. Does this picture imply that the longer one lives, the less one counts in the eyes of God? Obviously not. She does not push the picture in that direction. She is saluting her sons, that is all. Her practice is decisive. It need not be confused or superstitious. On the other hand, I do not find the picture very helpful. It sustained her, but it would not sustain me. Here, she and I have to speak for ourselves. (Phillips, 1993, p. 248)

Reactions to religious beliefs '*must* be personal', Phillips insists, for faith is a matter of personal reaction in which we all speak for ourselves. This is not a cause for regret or an opportunity for another's contemptuous dismissal. It is, rather, the mark of authentic God-talk.

If we engage in God-talk ourselves, we need to remember the old maxim to 'Watch your language.' Unless we reflect on what we are saying, our words may end up not saying anything at all; they can certainly mislead others about what we really believe. And 'careless talk', as the old wartime posters put it, can 'cost lives'. But this does not mean that we should stifle our religious talk, and it surely doesn't mean that we should be so ready to correct the God-talk of others that they are shamed into total silence.

Most (if not perhaps all?) who speak of and to God need to be encouraged to say more, and so to say it better. In God's name, then, *talk*.

Further reading

Astley, J (2002), *Ordinary Theology: looking, listening and learning in theology*, Aldershot, Ashgate, chapter 4.

Cupitt, D (1991), *What is a Story?*, London, SCM.

Grey, M (2001), *Introducing Feminist Images of God*, Sheffield, Sheffield Academic Press.

Holdsworth, J (2003), *Communication and the Gospel*, London, Darton, Longman and Todd.

Liturgical Commission (1993), *Language and the Worship of the Church*, London, General Synod of the Church of England (GS 1115).

McFague, S (1983), *Metaphorical Theology: models of God in religious language*, London, SCM, chapter 5.

Slee, N (2003), *Faith and Feminism: an introduction to Christian feminist theology*, London, Darton, Longman and Todd.

Slee, N (2004), *Women's Faith Development: patterns and processes*, Aldershot, Ashgate.

White, S J (1997), *Groundwork of Christian Worship*, Peterborough, Epworth, pp. 193–197.

Wren, B (1989), *What Language Shall I Borrow? God-talk in worship: a male response to feminist theology*, London, SCM.

REFERENCES

Alston, W P (1987), Functionalism and theological language, in T V Morris (ed.), *The Concept of God*, chapter 1, Oxford, Oxford University Press.

Alston, W P (1989), *Divine Nature and Human Language: essays in philosophical theology*, Ithaca, New York, Cornell University Press.

Anderson, J F (1949), *The Bond of Being*, St Louis, Missouri, Herder.

Aquinas (1963-1975), *Summa Theologiae*, ed. T Gilby, London, Eyre and Spottiswoode (60 vols).

Astley, J (1981), The 'indispensability' of the incarnation, *King's Theological Review*, IV, 1, 15–21.

Astley, J (1992), Christian worship and the hidden curriculum of Christian learning, in J Astley and D Day (eds), *The Contours of Christian Education*, pp. 141–152, Great Wakering, McCrimmons.

Astley, J (2000a), *God's World*, London, Darton, Longman and Todd.

Astley, J (ed.) (2000b), *Learning in the Way: research and reflection on adult Christian education*, Leominster, Gracewing.

Astley, J (2002), *Ordinary Theology: looking, listening and learning in theology*, Aldershot, Ashgate.

Astley, J; Francis, L J and Crowder, C (eds) (1996), *Theological Perspectives on Christian Formation: a reader*, Leominster, Gracewing.

Austin, J L (1962), *How to Do Things with Words*, Oxford, Oxford University Press.

Austin, J L (1970), *Philosophical Papers*, Oxford, Oxford University Press.

Avis, P (1999), *God and the Creative Imagination: metaphor, symbol and myth in religion and theology*, London, Routledge.

Ayer, A J (1946), *Language, Truth and Logic*, London, Victor Gollancz.

von Balthasar, H U (1989), *The Word Made Flesh*, ET San Francisco, Ignatius Press.

Bailey, E (1997), *Implicit Religion in Contemporary Society*, Kampen, The Netherlands, Kok Pharos.

Banner, M C (1990), *The Justification of Science and the Rationality of Religious Belief*, Oxford, Oxford University Press.

Barbour, I G (1974), *Myths, Models and Paradigms: the nature of scientific and religious language*, London, SCM.

Barr, J (1981), *Fundamentalism*, London, SCM.

Barrett, C (1990), The language of ecstasy and the ecstasy of language, in M Warner (ed.), *The Bible as Rhetoric: studies in biblical persuasion and credibility*, pp. 205–221, London, Routledge.

Barrett, C (1991), *Wittgenstein on Ethics and Religious Belief*, Oxford, Blackwell.

Barth, K (1972), *Protestant Theology in the Nineteenth Century: its background and history*, ET London, SCM.

Barth, K (1975), *Church Dogmatics*, Vol. I/1, ET Edinburgh, T and T Clark.

Barthes, R (1977), *Image – Music – Text*, ET London, Collins.

Bausch, W J (1984), *Storytelling: imagination and faith*, Mystic, Connecticut, Twenty-Third Publications.

Black, M (1962), *Models and Metaphors: studies in language and philosophy*, Ithaca, New York, Cornell University Press.

Black, M (1979), More about metaphor, in A Ortony (ed.), *Metaphor and Thought*, pp. 19–43, Cambridge, Cambridge University Press.

Braithwaite, R B (1966), An empiricist's view of the nature of religious belief, in I T Ramsey (ed.), *Christian Ethics and Contemporary Philosophy*, pp. 53–73, London, SCM.

Braithwaite, R B (1968), *Scientific Explanation*, Cambridge, Cambridge University Press.

Brooks, C and Warren, R P (1976), *Understanding Poetry*, Austin, Texas, Holt, Rinehart and Winston.

Browning, D S (1991), *A Fundamental Practical Theology: descriptive and strategic proposals*, Minneapolis, Minnesota, Fortress.

Bultmann, R (1960), *Jesus Christ and Mythology*, London, SCM.

Bultmann, R (1964), New Testament and mythology, in H W Bartsch (ed.), *Kerygma and Myth: a theological debate*, pp. 1–44, ET London, SPCK.

Brümmer, V (1981), *Theology and Philosophical Inquiry: an introduction*, London, Macmillan.

Caird, G B (1980), *The Language and Imagery of the Bible*, London, Duckworth.

Caputo, J D (2001), *On Religion*, London, Routledge.

Carse, J P (1985), *The Silence of God*, New York, Macmillan.

Cartledge, M (2002), *Charismatic Glossolalia: an empirical-theological study*, Aldershot, Ashgate.

Clack, B R (1999), *An Introduction to Wittgenstein's Philosophy of Religion*, Edinburgh, Edinburgh University Press.

Clark, D (1982), *Between Pulpit and Pew: folk religion in a North Yorkshire fishing village*, Cambridge, Cambridge University Press.

Common Worship: services and prayers for the Church of England (2000), London, Church House Publishing.

Cragg, K (1981), 'According to the Scriptures': literacy and revelation, in M Wadsworth (ed.), *Ways of Reading the Bible*, pp. 23–37, Brighton, Harvester.

Crossan, J D (1975), *The Dark Interval: towards a theology of story*, Allen, Texas, Argus.

Cupitt, D (1980), *Taking Leave of God*, London, SCM.

Cupitt, D (1991), *What is a Story?*, London, SCM.

Cupitt, D (1998), *Mysticism after Modernity*, Oxford, Blackwell.

Cupitt, D (1999a), *The New Religion of Life in Everyday Speech*, London, SCM.

Cupitt, D (1999b), *The Meaning of it All in Everyday Speech*, London, SCM.

Cupitt, D (2001), *Emptiness and Brightness*, Santa Rosa, California, Polebridge.

Davies, B (1993), *An Introduction to the Philosophy of Religion*, Oxford, Oxford University Press.

Davis, C F (1989), *The Evidential Force of Religious Experience*, Oxford, Oxford University Press.

Derrida, J (1976), *Of Grammatology*, ET Baltimore, Maryland, John Hopkins University Press.

Derrida, J (1978), *Writing and Difference*, ET Chicago, University of Chicago Press.

Dickinson, E (1970), *The Complete Poems*, London, Faber and Faber.

Dillistone, F W (1983), Experience, religious, in A Richardson and J Bowden (eds), *A New Dictionary of Christian Theology*, pp. 204–207, London, SCM.

Drane, J (2000), *The McDonaldization of the Church: spirituality, creativity and the future of the church*, London, Darton, Longman and Todd.

Dunbar, R (1996), *Grooming, Gossip and the Evolution of Language*, London, Faber and Faber.

Evans, R (1999), *Using the Bible: studying the text*, London, Darton, Longman and Todd.

Farley, E (1983), *Theologia: the fragmentation and unity of theological education*, Philadelphia, Fortress.

Farley, E (1988), *The Fragility of Knowledge: theological education in the church and the university*, Philadelphia, Fortress.

Fawcett, T (1970), *The Symbolic Language of Religion*, London, SCM.

Flew, A G N and MacIntyre, A (eds) (1955), *New Essays in Philosophical Theology*, London, SCM.

Ford, D F (1999), *Theology: a very short introduction*, Oxford, Oxford University Press.

Fowler, J W (1981), *Stages of Faith: the psychology of human development and the quest for meaning*, San Francisco, Harper and Row.

Fowler, J and Keen, S (1978), *Life Maps: conversations on the journey of faith*, ed. J Berryman, Waco, Texas, Word.

Frei, H (1975), *The Identity of Jesus Christ: the hermeneutical bases of dogmatic theology*, Philadelphia, Fortress.

Frost, D L (1973), *The Language of Series 3*, Bramcote, Grove.

Gadamer, H-G (1993), *Truth and Method*, ET London, Sheed and Ward.

Gardiner, P (1988), *Kierkegaard*, Oxford, Oxford University Press.

Gill, R (1999), *Churchgoing and Christian Ethics*, Cambridge, Cambridge University Press.

Groome, T H (1980), *Christian Religious Education: sharing our story and vision*, San Francisco, Harper and Row.

Groome, T H (1991), *Sharing Faith: a comprehensive approach to religious education and pastoral ministry*, San Francisco, HarperSanFrancisco.

Gunton, C E (1988), *The Actuality of Atonement: a study of metaphor, rationality and the Christian tradition*, Edinburgh, T and T Clark.

Happold, F C (1970), *Mysticism: a study and an anthology*, Harmondsworth, Penguin.

Hardy, A C (1979), *The Spiritual Nature of Man: a study of contemporary religious experience*, Oxford, Oxford University Press.

Hare, R M (1992), *Essays in Religion and Education*, Oxford, Oxford University Press.

Harris, M (1991), *Teaching and Religious Imagination: an essay in the theology of teaching*, San Francisco, HarperSanFrancisco.

Hay, D (1982), *Exploring Inner Space: scientists and religious experience*, Harmondsworth, Penguin.

Hayner, P C (1958), Analogical predication, *Journal of Philosophy*, LV, 20, 1958, 855–862.

Hauerwas, S and Jones, L G (eds) (1989), *Why Narrative? Readings in narrative theology*, Grand Rapids, Michigan, Eerdmans.

Heidegger, M (1962), *Being and Time*, ET Oxford, Blackwell.

Heimbeck, R S (1969), *Theology and Meaning: a critique of metatheological scepticism*, London, George Allen and Unwin.

Hesse, M (1954), *Science and the Human Imagination*, London, SCM.

Hick, J (1973), *God and the Universe of Faiths*, London, Macmillan.

Holmer, P L (1978), *The Grammar of Faith*, San Francisco, Harper and Row.

Iser, W (1980), Interaction between text and reader, in S R Suleiman and I Crosman (eds), *The Reader in the Text: essays on audience and interpretation*, pp. 106–119, Princeton, NJ, Princeton University Press.

Jabusch, W F (1980), *The Person in the Pulpit: preaching as caring*, Nashville, Abingdon.

James, W (1960), *The Varieties of Religious Experience*, London, Collins.

Kellenberger, J (1985), *The Cognitivity of Religion: three perspectives*, London, Macmillan.

Kierkegaard, S (1941), *Concluding Unscientific Postscript*, ET Princeton, Princeton University Press.

Laurentin, R (1977), *Catholic Pentecostalism*, London, Darton, Longman and Todd.

Le Guin, U K (1989), *Dancing at the Edge of the World: thoughts on words, women, places*, New York, Grove.

Lindbeck, G A (1984), *The Nature of Doctrine: religion and theology in a postliberal age*, London, SPCK.

Luckmann, T (1967), *The Invisible Religion: the problem of religion in modern society*, New York, Macmillan.

Macquarrie, J (1967), *God-Talk: an examination of the language and logic of theology*, London, SCM.

Mascall, E L (1966), *Existence and Analogy*, London, Darton, Longman and Todd.

McCabe, H (1964), Analogy, in Aquinas, *Summa Theologiae*, Vol. 3, pp. 106–107.

McFague, S (1983), *Metaphorical Theology: models of God in religious language*, London, SCM.

Miles, T R (1972), *Religious Experience*, London, Macmillan.

Mitchell, B (ed.) (1971), *The Philosophy of Religion*, Oxford, Oxford University Press.

Moore, G (1988), *Believing in God: a philosophical essay*, Edinburgh, T and T Clark.

Morgan, R with Barton, J (1988), *Biblical Interpretation*, Oxford, Oxford University Press.

Murdoch, I (1970), *The Sovereignty of Good*, London, Routledge and Kegan Paul.

Nielsen, K (1982), *An Introduction to the Philosophy of Religion*, London, Macmillan.

Otto, R (1925), *The Idea of the Holy: an inquiry into the non-rational factor in the idea of the divine and its relation to the rational*, ET Oxford, Oxford University Press.

Palmer, H (1973), *Analogy: a study of qualification and argument in theology*, London, Macmillan.

Pattison, G (1997), *Kierkegaard and the Crisis of Faith: an introduction to his thought*, London, SPCK.

Pattison, G (1998), *The End of Theology and the Task of Thinking about God*, London, SCM.

Phillips, D Z (1965), *The Concept of Prayer*, London, Routledge and Kegan Paul.

Phillips, D Z (1967), Faith, scepticism and religious understanding, in D Z Phillips (ed.), *Religion and Understanding*, pp. 63–79, Oxford, Blackwell.

Phillips, D Z (1976), *Religion Without Explanation*, Oxford, Blackwell.

Phillips, D Z (1986), *Belief, Change and Forms of Life*, London, Macmillan.

Phillips, D Z (1993), *Wittgenstein and Religion*, Basingstoke, Macmillan.

Phillips, D Z (2001), *Religion and the Hermeneutics of Contemplation*, Cambridge, Cambridge University Press.

Pinker, S (1994), *The Language Instinct: the new science of language and mind*, London, Penguin.

Ramsey, I T (1957), *Religious Language: an empirical placing of theological phrases*, London, SCM.

Ramsey, I T (1963), Theological literacy, *The Chicago Theological Seminary Register*, 53, 5, 1–40.

Ramsey, I T (1964a), History and the gospels: some philosophical reflections, *Studia Evangelica*, III, 6, 201–219.

Ramsey, I T (1964b), *Models and Mystery*, Oxford, Oxford University Press.

Ramsey, I T (ed.) (1971a), *Words about God: the philosophy of religion*, London, SCM.

Ramsey, I T (1971b), *Our Understanding of Prayer*, London, SPCK.

Richards, I A (1936), *The Philosophy of Rhetoric*, Oxford, Oxford University Press.

Ricoeur, P (1969), *The Symbolism of Evil*, ET Boston, Beacon.

Ricoeur, P (1970), *Freud and Philosophy: an essay on interpretation*, ET New Haven, Connecticut, Yale University Press.

Ricoeur, P (1980), *Essays in Biblical Interpretation*, Philadelphia, Fortress.

Ricoeur, P (1981), *Hermeneutics and the Human Sciences*, ET Cambridge, Cambridge University Press.

Robinson, E (ed.) (1977), *The Original Vision: a study of the religious experience of childhood*, Oxford, Religious Experience Research Unit.

Ross, J (1998), Religious language, in B Davies (ed.), *Philosophy of Religion: a guide to the subject*, pp. 106–135, London, Cassell.

Ryle, G (1963), *The Concept of Mind*, Harmondsworth, Penguin.

Sauter, G and Barton, J (eds) (2000), *Revelation and Story: narrative theology and the centrality of story*, Aldershot, Ashgate.

Schleiermacher, F (1928), *The Christian Faith*, ET Edinburgh, T and T Clark.

Schleiermacher, F (1958), *On Religion: speeches to its cultured despisers*, ET New York, Harper and Row.

Slee, N (2003), *Faith and Feminism: an introduction to Christian feminist theology*, London, Darton, Longman and Todd.

Slee, N (2004), *Women's Faith Development: patterns and processes*, Aldershot, Ashgate.

Smart, N (1969), *Philosophers and Religious Truth*, London, SCM.

Smart, N (1972), *The Concept of Worship*, London, Macmillan.

Smart, N (1973), *The Phenomenon of Religion*, London, Macmillan.

Smart, N (1979), *The Philosophy of Religion*, London, Sheldon.

Smart, N (1996), *Dimensions of the Sacred: an anatomy of the world's beliefs*, London, HarperCollins.

Smart, N and Konstantine, S (1991), *Christian Systematic Theology in a World Context*, London, HarperCollins.

Soskice, J M (1985), *Metaphor and Religious Language*, Oxford, Oxford University Press.

Spinks, B D (1991), The eucharistic prayer, in K Stevenson and D Spinks (eds), *The Identity of Anglican Worship*, pp. 89–102, London, Mowbray.

Stace, W T (1960), *Mysticism and Philosophy*, London, Macmillan.

Stiver, D R (1996), *The Philosophy of Religious Language: sign, symbol and story*, Oxford, Blackwell.

Stiver, D R (2001), *Theology after Ricoeur: new directions in hermeneutical theology*, Louisville, Kentucky, John Knox.

Streng, F J (1978), Language and mystical awareness, in S T Katz (ed.), *Mysticism and Philosophical Analysis*, pp. 141–169, New York, Oxford University Press.

Swinburne, R (1977), *The Coherence of Theism*, Oxford, Oxford University Press.

Swinburne, R (1992), *Revelation: from metaphor to analogy*, Oxford, Oxford University Press.

Sykes, S W (1979), The incarnation as the foundation of the Church, in M Goulder (ed.), *Incarnation and Myth: the debate continues*, pp. 113–127, London, SCM.

Sykes, S W (1983), Theology, in A Richardson and J Bowden (eds), *A New Dictionary of Christian Theology*, pp. 566–567, London, SCM.

Tannen, D (1992), *You Just Don't Understand: women and men in conversation*, London, Virago.

Tennyson, A (1916), *Poetical Works of Alfred Lord Tennyson*, London, Macmillan.

TeSelle, S M (1975), *Speaking in Parables: a study in metaphor and theology*, London, SCM.

Thiselton, A C (1980), *The Two Horizons: New Testament hermeneutics and philosophical description with special reference to Heidegger, Bultmann, Gadamer, and Wittgenstein*, Exeter, Paternoster.

Thomas, R S (1993), *Collected Poems 1945-1990*, London, Orion.

Tinsley, J (1996), Tell it Slant, in J Astley, L J Francis and C Crowder (eds), *Theological Perspectives on Christian Formation: a reader in theology and Christian education*, pp. 88–94, Leominster, Gracewing Fowler Wright and Grand Rapids, Michigan, Eerdmans.

Tracy, D (1981), *The Analogical Imagination: Christian theology and the culture of pluralism*, London, SCM.

Underhill, E (1936), *Worship*, London, Nisbet.

Village, A (2003), *Biblical Interpretation among Church of England Lay People*, unpublished PhD thesis, University of Bristol.

Wainwright, G (1980), *Doxology: the praise of God in worship, doctrine and life*, London, Epworth.

Ward, J N (1967), *The Use of Praying*, London, Epworth.

Ward, K (1994), *Religion and Revelation: a theology of revelation in the world's religions*, Oxford, Oxford University Press.

Westerhoff, J H (1983), *Building God's People in a Materialistic Society*, New York, Seabury.

White, R (1982), Notes on analogical predication and speaking about God, in B Hebblethwaite and S Sutherland (eds), *The Philosophical Foundations of Theology*, pp. 197–226, Cambridge, Cambridge University Press.

Wilder, A N (1964), *Early Christian Rhetoric: the language of the gospel*, London, SCM.

Wiles, M (1977), Myth in theology, in J Hick (ed.), *The Myth of God Incarnate*, pp. 148–166, London, SCM.

Williams, R (2000a), *On Christian Theology*, Oxford, Blackwell.

Williams, R (2000b), *Lost Icons: reflections on cultural bereavement*, Edinburgh, T and T Clark.

Williams, R (2001), Making moral decisions, in R Gill (ed.), *The Cambridge Companion to Christian Ethics*, pp. 3–15, Cambridge, Cambridge University Press.

Wittgenstein, L (1966), *Lectures and Conversations on Aesthetics, Psychology and Religious Belief*, Oxford, Blackwell.

Wittgenstein, L (1967), *Zettel*, ET Oxford, Blackwell.

Wittgenstein, L (1968), *Philosophical Investigations*, ET Oxford, Blackwell.

Wittgenstein, L (1974), *On Certainty*, ET Oxford, Blackwell.

Wittgenstein, L (1980), *Culture and Value*, Oxford, Blackwell.

Wolterstorff, N (1995), *Divine Discourse: philosophical reflections on the claim that God speaks*, Cambridge, Cambridge University Press.

Zaehner, R C (1957), *Mysticism: sacred and profane*, Oxford, Oxford University Press.

GLOSSARY AND BIOGRAPHY

affections/affective feelings and emotions

agnosticism the condition of not knowing (especially about God)

algorithm rules for calculation (as in a computer program)

allegory a story in which the meaning or message is represented symbolically

analogy partial similarity

analogy of being the similarity between creatures and their Creator

analogy of faith knowing God's attributes through God's revelation

anthropocentric regarding human beings as central

anthropomorphic attributing human form or personality to the divine

Aquinas, St Thomas (1225–1274) Dominican philosopher and theologian

Aristotle (384–322 BC) Greek philosopher

atonement the act of reconciliation between humankind and God

Augustine, St (354–430) theologian and Bishop of Hippo (North Africa)

Austin, John L (1911–1960) English philosopher

Ayer, Alfred J (1910–1989) English philosopher

Barth, Karl (1886–1968) Swiss theologian

Braithwaite, Richard (1900–1990) English moral philosopher and philosopher of science

Bultmann, Rudolf (1884–1976) German New Testament scholar

Calvin, John (1509–1564) French Protestant Reformer

Carlyle, Thomas (1795–1881) Scottish historian and political philosopher

cognitive factual, truth-claiming *or* knowing, thinking, perceiving

Critical Theory a philosophy that sees social and cultural imperfections as defects of rationality

demythologising re-interpreting the mythical elements of a narrative (usually as claims about human life)

Dionysius/Pseudo-Dionysius unknown writer of the fifth and sixth centuries AD, who stressed the inadequacy of human language to portray the divine

empirical/empiricist focused on or known in sense experience; confirmable by sense experience

Enlightenment, the intellectual movement that emphasised experience and reason, and mistrusted authority and revelation

Eucharist Lord's Supper, Holy Communion or Mass: a church service that re-enacts the Last Supper

existential a philosophical position stressing the unique significance of concrete human existence and free human actions

figurative not literal (*see below*)

Flaubert, Gustave (1821–1880) French novelist and writer of short stories

form of life way of behaving

Gadamer, Hans-George (1900–2002) German philosopher

Heidegger, Martin (1889–1976) German philosopher

hermeneutics (the theory of) interpretation

ideology wide-ranging system of beliefs and values, sometimes thought to be distorted and to serve political purposes

immanence indwelling; God's all-pervading presence

inerrant without error

intuition insight that is not based on reasoning

John of the Cross, St (1549–1591) Spanish mystic and poet

Kierkegaard, Søren (1813–1855) Danish existentialist philosopher

language game a rule-governed linguistic practice

literal taking words in their usual sense

Locke, John (1632–1704) English empirical philosopher

metaphor a figure of speech used to speak about one thing in terms that suggests another thing

myth significant narratives about the behaviour of divine beings

nihilism theory promoting absence of allegiance or sense of purpose; 'believing in nothing'

non-cognitive involving no cognition or knowledge; neither true nor false

non-realism the denial of realism (*see below*)

Otto, Rudolf (1869–1937) German scholar

parable stories drawn from common life which carry significant meanings

patriarchal relating to/assuming male leadership

piety quality of being devout (reverent, religious)

phenomenology description of actual experience

Popper, Karl R (1902–1994) Viennese philosopher of science, taught in London

positivism/logical positivism the view that sense experience is the only form of factual knowledge; rejection of metaphysics

post-liberalism theological movement that treats Christianity as essentially a matter of embracing a tradition and learning the language of faith

post-modernism rejection of Enlightenment notions of one truth, narrative or rationality; playful and eclectic embracing of plurality and relativism

praxis reflective action

predestination the belief that God ordains from eternity our actions or salvation

predicate/predication the description of something in terms of some property, activity or relationship

proposition that which is proposed or stated

Ramsey, Ian (1915–1972) English philosopher of religion and Bishop of Durham

realism the belief that reality exists independently of human language and experience

relativism the view that truth is relative to the standpoint of the judging subject, and is therefore not absolute

Romantic Movement/Romanticism movement of thought that emphasised creativity and human feeling over against reason

Schleiermacher, Friedrich D E (1768–1834) German Liberal Protestant theologian

secular non-religious (or, sometimes, anti-religious) stances or phenomena

simile a figure of speech in which one thing is explicitly compared with something else

Smart, Ninian (1927–2001) Scottish philosopher of religion and champion of religious studies

speech acts the social acts performed in and by saying or writing something

Synoptic gospels Matthew, Mark and Luke – three gospels that have a similar 'viewpoint' on Jesus, and share close textual similarities with one another

Temple, William (1881–1944) Anglican theologian and Archbishop of Canterbury

Teresa of Avila, St (1512–1582) Spanish Carmelite nun and mystic

Tillich, Paul (1888–1965) German-American philosopher of religion

Tinsley, John (1919–1992) English theologian and Bishop of Bristol

transcendence surpassing experience, language or thought; 'otherness'; God's radical difference from all other (created) realities

trope a figurative use of a word or phrase

via negativa the use of negation to speak of God; (in mysticism) self-emptying

Wittgenstein, Ludwig (1889–1951) philosopher of language, born in Austria but taught in Cambridge

INDEX OF THEMES

thanksgiving 28–29
theological listening 126–127
theology 3–8 *see also* academic
    theology, ordinary theology, reli-
    gious and theological language
theology from below 17, 21
tradition 106
transcendence 13, 18–20, 57–58
truth 48–49, 51–63, 67–77

union 20–21
univocal language 56–57, 61–63
unselfing 25–26
use as meaning 84, 89

variety of religious language 2–10,
    95–97
verification 67–68
via negativa/negative theology 57 *see*
    also apophasis

wisdom 5, 63
worship 3, 6, 24–33, 100–102